the simple guide to LABRADOR RETRIEVERS

Sheila Webster Boneham, PhD.

T.F.H. Publications, Inc.

T.F.H. Publications, Inc.
One TFH Plaza
Third and Union Avenues
Neptune City, NJ 07753

Printed and Bound in China
07 08 09 3 5 7 9 8 6 4 2

ISBN 978-079382113-6

The Leader In Responsible Animal Care For Over 50 Years!™
www.tfhpublications.com
CENTRAL
Garden & Pet

Contents

Household Hazards Page 48

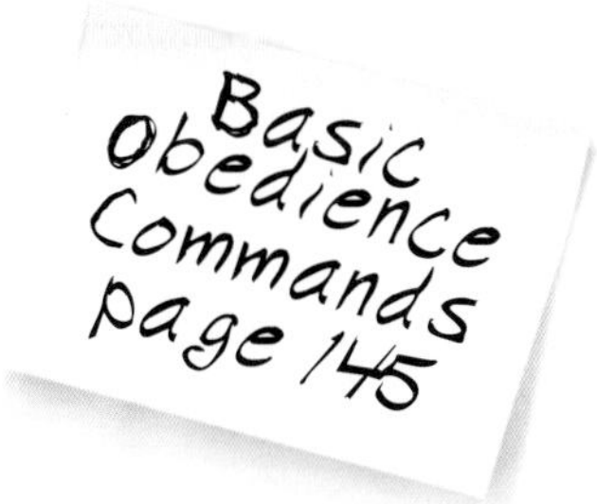
Basic
Obedience
Commands
page 145

Part One

Introducing The Labrador Retriever

1

Introducing the Labrador Retriever

It's no great mystery why the Labrador Retriever has held the rank of most popular breed with the American Kennel Club (AKC) since 1991. For his fans, the well-bred Lab is as close to perfection as mortal dog can be–beautiful, athletic, kind, cheerful, loyal, friendly, intelligent, and versatile.

For over a decade, the Labrador Retriever has been the most popular breed of dog with the AKC.

The Lab is a medium to large dog, ideally standing $21\frac{1}{2}$ to $24\frac{1}{2}$ inches tall at the withers (the highest point of the shoulders), with dogs (males) tending to be slightly taller than bitches (females). In working condition, the Lab weighs from 55 to 80 pounds.

Every breed of dog is distinguished by traits

The Labrador Retriever originated in Newfoundland, not Labrador as the name suggests.

typical of the breed. The well-bred Labrador Retriever is easy to recognize by specifically Labrador traits. He has a short, dense "double" coat consisting of a downy undercoat for warmth and a courser outer coat that repels water. The Lab's perpetually wagging tail is distinctive. Known as an "otter" tail, it's thick at the base, round and tapering to the tip, with the hair lying flat without a "flag." The Labrador Retriever's head should be clean-cut and broad across the skull, and there should be a moderate "stop," or indentation where the muzzle joins the skull. Because the Lab was bred to retrieve and carry large game fowl in water and fields, he has powerful jaws but a "soft" mouth that doesn't damage the birds. Perhaps most endearing are the Lab's soft, friendly eyes and cheerful expression, which communicates his honest character, intelligence, good temperament, and joyful attitude. Does the Labrador Retriever sound too good to be true? If so, hold on–Labs are definitely *not* perfect for everyone. Why not? We can find the answer by looking at the history of the breed and what it means for modern-day Labs and their people.

Did You Know?

All breeds of domestic dogs were bred for specific purposes. Breeders create and sustain breeds by breeding animals that possess the physical and behavioral traits the breeders prefer. If you're looking for a dog to do a job, you'll do better with a breed that was developed for that purpose. What does that have to do with choosing a dog just for companionship? A lot! The traits that breeders have selected and strengthened in creating the breed will be there whether you want them or not. It is those highly predictable traits, in fact, that make a breed a *breed*.

A Brief History of the Labrador Retriever

Origins

The Labrador Retriever originated in Newfoundland, not Labrador as the name suggests. Initially, in fact, the breed was known as the "lesser Newfoundland," "lesser" referring to its smaller size when compared to the giant "greater" Newfoundland.

Archeologists have found no evidence that the Indians native to Newfoundland kept dogs. On the contrary, domestic canines seem to have arrived on the coast of Newfoundland with European fishermen who used the dogs to drag nets and small boats in the water and to retrieve fish. In 1662, W.E.

Cormack, a native of St. John's, walked across Newfoundland and kept a journal of his travels. He writes there about dogs "admirably trained as retrievers in fowling and…otherwise useful." The dogs he describes were small enough for fishermen to carry in their dories, and had short, dense coats that did not collect ice and encumber the dogs in cold weather. According to Labrador breeder and judge Bernard Ziessow, Labrador Retrievers were still used in Newfoundland to retrieve fish as late as the 1920s.

British sportsmen were impressed with the Lab's swimming and retrieving abilities.

During the 19th century, the range and accuracy of firearms improved, and the sport of shooting birds on the wing became popular. Since the birds often fell into water or heavy brush some distance from the hunter, dogs with a natural inclination to find and bring back the birds were clearly of value. Initially, the word "retriever" indicated function and referred to any dog that retrieved on command, regardless of what breed or combination of breeds it was.

British sportsmen were impressed by the swimming and retrieving abilities and amiable temperament of the Lesser Newfoundland, or "St. John's Dog," and dogs began returning to Britain, the land of their forebears. The third Earl of Malmsbury, along with his father, imported some of the first St. John's or Labrador dogs to Britain and bred them during the 19th century. In 1887, he wrote, "We always call mine Labrador dogs and I have kept the breed as pure as I could from the first I had–the real breed may be known by their having a close coat which turns water off like oil, and, about all, a tail like an otter."

While the Earl of Malmsbury was developing his Labrador dogs, three other fanciers–the fifth Duke of Buccleugh, Lord John Scott, and the tenth Earl of Home–began a similar breeding venture, developing the Buccleugh line. The eleventh Lord of Home continued the breeding program, but by the time of his death in 1881, the line was nearly extinct. A year later, the third Earl of Malmsbury happened to meet the sixth Duke of Buccleugh and the twelfth Earl of Home. He gave them some of the dogs from his own lines, and the

Buccleugh line was revived and the breed brought into the 20th century. Buccleugh's Ned and Buccleugh's Avon are generally regarded as ancestors of all modern Labrador retrievers.

Did You Know?

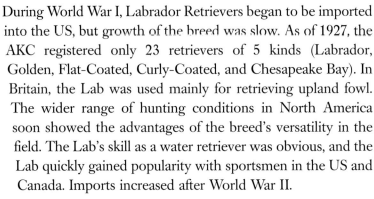

The Labrador Retriever was first recognized as a distinct breed by the Kennel Club (England) on July 7, 1903. The American Kennel Club (AKC) recognized the Labrador Retriever in 1917.

The similarity of the two lines of dogs, bred independently from one another for some fifty years, suggests that both kennels selected for traits very close to those of the original St. John's Dog. Other influential kennels were established during the early 20th century. Most early breeders bred for a sound, intelligent, working retriever in a correctly conformed body, and there were many Dual Champions–dogs that earned both field and show championships–at that time.

Labs were imported into the US during World War I.

Home to North America

During World War I, Labrador Retrievers began to be imported into the US, but growth of the breed was slow. As of 1927, the AKC registered only 23 retrievers of 5 kinds (Labrador, Golden, Flat-Coated, Curly-Coated, and Chesapeake Bay). In Britain, the Lab was used mainly for retrieving upland fowl. The wider range of hunting conditions in North America soon showed the advantages of the breed's versatility in the field. The Lab's skill as a water retriever was obvious, and the Lab quickly gained popularity with sportsmen in the US and Canada. Imports increased after World War II.

It wasn't long before the Lab's kind nature, joyful attitude, trainability, and overall value as a companion were noticed by the public, and the Lab wagged its way into homes where its primary value is as a pet, a playmate, and an occasional pillow. Many Labrador Retrievers serve society as guide dogs for the blind, service dogs, and therapy dogs. Others have distinguished themselves in the tough and dangerous field of search and rescue, and still others work with law enforcement to detect explosives, narcotics, and arson.

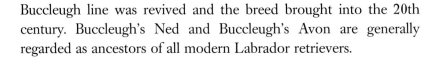

Yellow Labs and Golden Retrievers

Yellow Labrador Retrievers are often erroneously called "golden Labs." There is only one correct term for Labrador Retrievers ranging in color from very pale cream through gold to dark fox-red, and that term is *yellow*.

The Golden Retriever is an entirely separate breed from the Labrador Retriever.

Yellow Labs have been part of the breed since early on, but in the early days of the breed's development, yellow puppies were routinely culled. The first yellow Labrador Retriever to be registered was Ben of Hyde. Fortunately, the prejudice against yellows eventually died, and today there are many high-quality yellows in the field, and in the conformation, obedience, and agility rings.

Today, there are two major styles of Labrador Retrievers in North America: "field bred" and "show bred." Although there is variation within both styles, field-bred Labs, because they come from breeding animals selected for their hunting or field-trialing abilities, tend to have a lot of drive and energy. They also tend to be a bit taller and leaner than show-bred Labs. Show lines, in contrast, tend to be bred for conformation and temperament rather than working ability, although most show-bred Labs have some working instinct. In addition, there are far too many Labs bred with no purpose at all except to have puppies and make money for their owners. These "backyard bred" or puppy mill Labs often lack the physical and mental traits that made the breed so popular in the first place. It's especially troubling to find temperament problems, since one of the main virtues of a good Lab is its wonderful disposition. That's why it's to the buyer's advantage to buy from a serious breeder.

The Best Environment for a Lab

Unfortunately, people sometimes choose a dog by looking only at its virtues. It's important to remember that the Lab was bred to work long days retrieving fowl, often in cold, wet weather and rugged terrain. In order to work well and happily in such conditions, a dog needs to have nearly inexhaustible energy, a high pain threshold, and the ability to solve problems on his own. When those traits are understood and properly managed with exercise, training, and a sense of humor, they are highly desirable. When mismanaged, the same traits are a liability, and all too many Labs find their way into rescue programs and shelters (or worse) because of the very traits for which the breed is renowned.

The Labrador Retriever is a high-energy breed and needs positive outlets to release it.

High energy means *more* energy than some people can or want to deal with. A 70-pound whirling dervish of a young, happy Lab is a handful, and most Lab owners have suffered bonks and bruises from a Lab in "crazy dog" mode. Pent-up energy coupled with boredom can make for annoying and destructive behaviors like barking, digging, jumping, and chewing, so Lab owners must find ways to channel their dogs' energy and intelligence. The normal high energy of a young Lab is often wrongly labeled hyperactivity. Unfortunately, there are hyperactive Labs, but they tend to be bred by people with little knowledge of genetics who don't select for parents with proper temperament. Still, the fact is that Labs, especially Lab puppies and adolescents, are exuberant, and too often people are unprepared for that very normal behavior.

The Labrador Retriever's high tolerance for discomfort makes him a challenge to manage at times, since he may not even notice a tug on his leash that would make a more physically sensitive dog stop in its tracks. On the other hand, Labs are people-oriented and they want to please us, and positive methods of training work very well with them. Intelligence and problem-solving ability are terrific when channeled into sports, tricks, and other productive pursuits, but left undirected, they make for escape artists and unsolicited home and garden re-designers.

Lab pups love being with their owners and with other dogs.

A well-bred Labrador Retriever is very stable emotionally, and will take most things in stride. These are loving, social dogs, and they are happiest when they are with their family. Relegating a Lab to isolation in the back yard is not only shameful, but will lead to such problem behaviors as barking or digging in most cases. Labs are usually very patient

Rare Colors?

What about "rare" colors? Buyer, beware! Anyone offering "rare" colors for high prices is running a scam. They are either ignorant of ethical breeding practices and Labrador genetics, or they don't care. Either way, you're well advised to steer clear of them.

The only correct colors in the Labrador Retriever are black, yellow, and chocolate.

Some yellow Labs are very pale, almost white, but they are still considered to be yellows, and most have some color on the tips of their ears or elsewhere. Similarly, "fox red" is simply a dark, sandy-red and is considered to be a shade of yellow. Neither the pale nor the dark yellows are "rare."

"Silver" Labradors are either crosses with Weimaraners or very light chocolates. In the first case, the dog is *not* purebred, and in the second case, it is a mismark. Either way, it should definitely not command a higher price!

A cute Lab puppy doesn't stay small for long.

with children, but children also need to be taught to respect the dog, and interaction between young children and *any* dog should be closely supervised. Although some Labs will bark protectively and some are a bit territorial, they are not guard dogs–most Labs will welcome newcomers with joyful enthusiasm.

Labs can be messy, and are probably not the best choice of canine companion for a fastidious housekeeper. Their happy tails can clear a coffee table. Their rambunctious style of play and "life is a contact sport" attitude can send furniture flying. Dog hair is part of life with Labs. They are moderate shedders most of the year, but in the fall, and especially the spring, they "blow" their coats, shedding lots of spiky little hairs that insert themselves into carpets, upholstery, and clothes. Your vacuum cleaner will get lots of exercise!

Are You a Labrador Retriever Person? A Ten Question Test

1. Do you have a sense of humor?
2. Are you comfortable living with dog hair in your house and car?
3. Do you have time to spend at least an hour a day exercising your dog when he's young?
4. Can you live with the occasional chewed-up woodwork or shoe?
5. Are you comfortable with a big dog following you from room to room just to be with you?
6. Do you like big wet doggy kisses?
7. Can you live without lots of knickknacks at tail height on coffee and end tables?
8. Are you physically healthy and strong enough to manage a rambunctious 70-pound dog that thinks life is a contact sport?
9. Do you have 10 or 12 years to be the reason-to-live for a dog?
10. Does your soul take flight when you gaze into deep, dark canine eyes?

If you answered yes to at least eight of these questions, you may indeed be a Labrador Person!

Brushing once or twice a week–more while the dog is blowing its coat in spring and fall–will help minimize hair in the house. But make no mistake–there will be hair! Labs love to play in mud and water, and some are diggers who make a mess of the yard and themselves–and, on occasion, carpets, floors, upholstery, and bedspreads.

So before you rush to join the ranks of Lab owners, please think carefully about the whole dog, not just the sweet guy you picture sitting at your feet by the fire. It takes both a dog and a person or family to make a lasting canine-human relationship, and the would-be owner's traits are at least as important as those of the dog. For everyone's sake, be realistic and choose carefully.

Temperament

The Labrador Retriever's happy, friendly, stable temperament is perhaps his greatest virtue, and undoubtedly the main reason that he has held first place in the hearts of so many people for so long. But good temperament is no accident. If breeders do not select breeding dogs based on proper temperament as well as other traits, it will be lost.

Part 1

Unfortunately, the rise of the Lab to star status as a companion has prompted some irresponsible breeders to breed any dogs capable of reproducing. Many such Labs have terrible temperaments (as well as health problems), exhibiting problems ranging from aggression to shyness to hyperactivity–none of which are correct or appropriate to this beautiful breed.

One reason the Labrador Retriever is so popular is his friendly, stable temperament.

Before you buy, meet the breeder's dogs. This will give you an idea of the dogs' general personalities, and also the energy level you should expect from these lines. Labs should be friendly, happy, playful, and outgoing, but controllable. Ask people who have purchased dogs from the breeder whether their dogs have exhibited any temperament problems. If you don't like what you see in the breeder's adult dogs, don't buy a puppy. Go elsewhere. There's no point in having a dog that's a Labrador Retriever in name only, but lacks the temperament and other traits that made you want a Lab in the first place.

The Breed Standard—Defining the Ideal Lab

A "breed standard" is a document created by members of a breed club to establish a set of characteristics that define a breed. In the US, the Labrador Retriever competes primarily in shows sanctioned by the AKC and governed by its rules. When Labs are shown in AKC conformation shows, they are judged against the standard established by the Labrador Retriever Club of America (LRC), which is the AKC "parent club" for the breed. The current breed standard became effective March 31, 1994.

The Official Standard for the Labrador Retriever

General Appearance–The Labrador Retriever is a strongly built, medium-sized, short-coupled, dog possessing a sound, athletic, well-balanced conformation that enables it to function as a retrieving gun dog; the substance and soundness to hunt waterfowl or upland game for long hours under difficult conditions; the character and quality to win in the

Key to Terms Used in the Labrador Retriever Breed Standard

Barrel chested—rounded chest in which the ribs curve out from the point of attachment to the spine

Brindle—color pattern in which darker hairs form bands or stripes on a background of tan, brown, or yellow

Brisket—chest; breastbone

Cow hocks—hocks turned inward

Crossing over—movement in which the front and/or back feet cross over one another and over an imaginary center line drawn in the direction of movement

Croup—muscular area above and around the place where the tail extends from the spine

Dewclaw—underdeveloped toe located on the inside of the leg above the foot

Ewe neck—neck that curves upward

Foreface—the portion of the skull in front of the brain case; the muzzle

Full dentition—a full adult compliment of 42 teeth

Hare feet—foot with little arching of the toes, and center toes considerably longer than outer toes.

Hock—joint on hind leg between thigh and pastern (lower leg); in many breed standards it is used to mean the entire rear pastern

Knuckling over—forward bending of the leg at the wrist joint

Level bite—commonly used to refer to bite in which the upper and lower incisors meet evenly when the mouth is closed; technically, bite in which the upper and lower jaws are equal in length.

Loaded—excessively developed, bulging muscles

Loin—lumbar area, between the end of the rib cage and the pelvis

Occipital bone—bony ridge at the back of the skull

Otter tail—strong tail, thick at the base and tapering to the tip, flat on the underside

Out at the elbows—movement in which the elbows point outward

Overangulation—too sharp an angle in the shoulder and/or hip joint

Overshot—bite in which the lower jaw recedes, so that the upper teeth are placed far forward of the equivalent lower teeth

Pacing—two-beat gait in which the legs on each side move in unison

Paddling—poor movement in which the forefeet make circles at each step

Pastern—region between the wrist and the foot in front, hock joint and foot in back.

Patella—kneecap

Point of shoulder—where the scapula (shoulder blade) meets the humerus (upper arm bone)

Scissors bite—bite in which the inner surfaces of the upper incisors meet the outer surfaces of the lower incisors when the mouth is shut.

Short-coupled—relatively short space between the last rib and the rear leg assembly.

Sickle hocks—pasterns (hocks) which angle forward from the hock joint to the foot.

Side-winding—(also called "crabbing") forward movement in which the spinal column is not aligned with the direction of travel

Slab-sided—flat ribs with no "spring," or curve

Snippiness—weak or pointed foreface

Spring of ribs—curve of the ribs

Stifle—knee joint

Stop—depression located between the eyes where the frontal bones of the skull meet the muzzle

Tied-in elbows—elbows turned in and held close to the ribs, causing the feet to be farther apart than the elbows when view from the front

Towline—top of the dog in profile

Tuck-up—upward sweep of the abdomen behind the rib cage

Underline—outline of the chest and abdomen in profile

Undershot—bite in which the lower jaw and teeth extend farther forward than the upper

Weaving—movement in which the feet cross in front of one another

Weedy—having bones that are too light and thin

Well balanced—proportioned symmetrically, particularly in reference to the angles of the shoulder and hip joints

Well laid back—shoulder blades set at about a 45-degree angle to the horizontal

Withers—the high point of the shoulder blades, just behind the neck show ring; and the temperament to be a family companion. Physical features and mental characteristics should denote a dog bred to perform as an efficient retriever of game with a stable temperament suitable for a variety of pursuits beyond the hunting environment.

The most distinguishing characteristics of the Labrador Retriever are its short, dense, weather resistant coat; an "otter" tail; a clean-cut head with broad back skull and moderate stop; powerful jaws; and its "kind," friendly eyes, expressing character, intelligence and good temperament.

Above all, a Labrador Retriever must be well balanced, enabling it to move in the show ring or work in the field with little or no effort. The typical Labrador possesses style and quality without over refinement, and substance without lumber or cloddiness. The Labrador is bred primarily as a working gun dog; structure and soundness are of great importance.

Size, Proportion and Substance–*Size*–The height at the withers for a dog is $22\frac{1}{2}$ to $24\frac{1}{2}$ inches; for a bitch is $21\frac{1}{2}$ to $23\frac{1}{2}$ inches. Any variance greater than $\frac{1}{2}$ inch above or below these heights is a disqualification. Approximate weight of dogs and bitches in working condition: dogs 65 to 80 pounds; bitches 55 to 70 pounds.

The correct height for a male Lab is $22\frac{1}{2}$ to $24\frac{1}{2}$ inches. A female is slightly smaller in height.

The minimum height ranges set forth in the paragraph above shall not apply to dogs or bitches under twelve months of age.

Proportion–Short-coupled; length from the point of the shoulder to the point of the rump is equal to or slightly longer than the distance from the withers to the ground. Distance from the elbow to the ground should be equal to one half of the height at the withers. The brisket should extend to the elbows, but not perceptibly deeper. The body must be of sufficient length to permit a straight, free and efficient stride; but the dog should never appear low and long or tall and leggy in outline.

Substance–Substance and bone proportionate to the overall dog. Light, "weedy" individuals are definitely incorrect; equally objectionable are cloddy lumbering specimens. Labrador Retrievers shall be shown in working condition well-muscled and without excess fat.

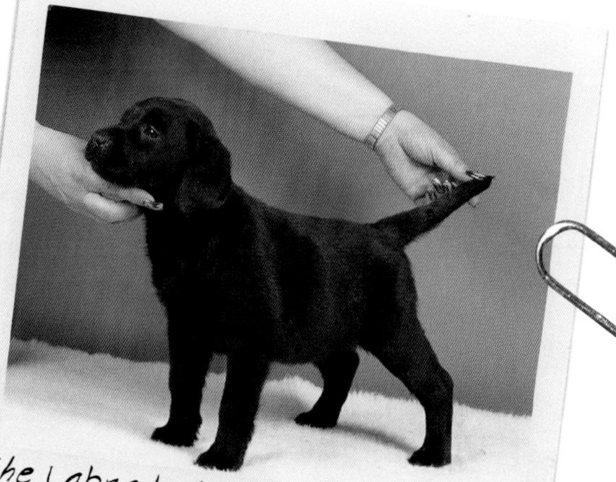

The Labrador's skull and foreface should be on parallel planes and of approximately equal length.

Head–*Skull*–The skull should be wide; well developed but without exaggeration. The skull and foreface should be on parallel planes and of approximately equal length. There should be a moderate stop–the brow slightly pronounced so that the skull is not absolutely in a straight line with the nose. The brow ridges aid in defining the stop. The head should be clean-cut and free from fleshy cheeks; the bony structure of the skull chiseled beneath the eye with no prominence in the cheek. The skull may show some median line; the occipital bone is not conspicuous in mature dogs. Lips should not be squared off or pendulous, but fall away in a curve toward the throat. A wedge-shape head, or a head long and narrow in muzzle and back skull is incorrect as are massive, cheeky heads. The jaws are powerful and free from snippiness–the muzzle neither long and narrow nor short and stubby. *Nose*–The nose should be wide and the nostrils well-developed. The nose should be black on black or yellow dogs, and brown on chocolates. Nose color fading to a lighter shade is not a fault. A thoroughly pink nose or one lacking in any pigment is a disqualification. *Teeth*–The teeth should be strong and regular with a scissors bite; the lower teeth just behind, but touching the inner side of the upper incisors. A level bite is acceptable, but not desirable. Undershot, overshot, or misaligned teeth are serious faults. Full dentition is preferred. Missing molars or pre-molars are serious faults. *Ears*–The ears should hang moderately close to the head, set rather far back, and somewhat low on the skull; slightly above eye level. Ears should not be large and heavy, but in proportion with the skull and reach to the inside of the eye when pulled forward. *Eyes*–Kind, friendly eyes imparting good temperament, intelligence and alertness are a hallmark of the breed. They should be of medium size, set well apart, and neither protruding nor deep set. Eye color should be brown in black and yellow Labradors, and brown or hazel in chocolates. Black, or yellow eyes give a harsh expression and are undesirable. Small eyes, set close together or round prominent eyes are not typical of the breed. Eye rims are black in black and yellow Labradors; and brown in chocolates. Eye rims without pigmentation is a disqualification.

Neck, Topline and Body–*Neck*–The neck should be of proper length to allow the dog to retrieve game easily. It should be muscular and free from throatiness. The neck should rise strongly from the shoulders with a moderate arch. A short, thick neck or a "ewe" neck is incorrect. *Topline*–The back is strong and the topline is level from the withers to the croup when standing or moving. However, the loin should show evidence of flexibility for athletic endeavor. *Body*–The Labrador should be short-coupled, with good spring of ribs tapering to a moderately wide chest. The Labrador should not be narrow chested; giving the appearance of hollowness between the front legs, nor should it have a wide spreading, bulldog-like front. Correct chest conformation will result in tapering between the front legs that allows unrestricted forelimb movement. Chest breadth that is either too wide or too narrow for efficient movement and stamina is incorrect. Slab-sided individuals are not typical of the breed; equally objectionable are rotund or barrel chested specimens. The underline is almost straight, with little or no tuck-up in mature animals. Loins should be short, wide and strong; extending to well developed, powerful hindquarters. When viewed from the side, the Labrador Retriever shows a well-developed, but not exaggerated forechest. *Tail*–The tail is a distinguishing feature of the breed. It should be very thick at the base, gradually tapering toward the tip, of medium length, and extending no longer than to the hock. The tail should be free from feathering and clothed thickly all around with the Labrador's short, dense coat, thus having that peculiar rounded appearance that has been described as the "otter" tail. The tail should follow the topline in repose or when in motion. It may be carried gaily, but should not curl over the back. Extremely short tails or long thin tails are serious faults. The tail completes the balance of the Labrador by giving it a flowing line from the top of the head to the tip of the tail. Docking or otherwise altering the length or natural carriage of the tail is a disqualification.

The tail should be very thick at the base and taper toward the tip.

Forequarters–Forequarters should be muscular, well coordinated and balanced with the hindquarters. *Shoulders*–The shoulders are well laid–back, long and sloping, forming an angle with the upper arm of approximately 90 degrees that permits the dog to move his forelegs in an easy manner with strong forward reach. Ideally, the length of the shoulder blade should equal the length of the upper arm. Straight shoulder blades, short upper arms or heavily muscled or loaded shoulders, all restricting free movement, are incorrect. *Front Legs*–When viewed from the front, the legs should be straight with good strong bone. Too much bone is as undesirable as too little bone, and short legged, heavy boned individuals are not typical of the breed. Viewed from the side, the elbows should be directly under the withers, and the front legs should be perpendicular to the ground and well under the body. The elbows should be close to the ribs without looseness. Tied-in elbows or being "out at the elbows" interfere with free movement and are serious faults. Pasterns should be strong and short and should slope slightly from the perpendicular line of the leg. Feet are strong and compact, with well-arched toes and well-developed pads. Dew claws may be removed. Splayed feet, hare feet, knuckling over, or feet turning in or out are serious faults.

Hindquarters–The Labrador's hindquarters are broad, muscular and well-developed from the hip to the hock with well-turned stifles and strong short hocks. Viewed from the rear, the hind legs are straight and parallel. Viewed from the side, the angulation of the rear legs is in balance with the front. The hind legs are strongly boned, muscled with moderate angulation at the stifle, and powerful, clearly defined thighs. The stifle is strong and there is no slippage of the patellae while in motion or when standing. The hock joints are strong, well let down and do not slip or hyper-extend while in motion or when standing. Angulation of both stifle and hock joint is such as to achieve the optimal balance of drive and traction. When standing the rear toes are only slightly behind the point of the rump. Over angulation produces a sloping topline not typical of the breed. Feet are strong and compact, with well-arched toes and well-developed pads. Cow-hocks, spread hocks, sickle hocks and over-angulation are serious structural defects and are to be faulted.

Coat–The coat is a distinctive feature of the Labrador Retriever. It should be short, straight and very dense, giving a fairly hard feeling to the hand. The Labrador should have a soft, weather-resistant undercoat that provides protection from water, cold and all types of ground cover. A slight wave down the back is permissible. Woolly coats, soft silky coats, and sparse slick coats are not typical of the breed, and should be severely penalized.

The Lab has a short, straight, very dense coat with a soft, weather-resistant undercoat.

Color–The Labrador Retriever coat colors are black, yellow and chocolate. Any other color or a combination of colors is a disqualification. A small white spot on the chest is permissible, but not desirable. White hairs from aging or scarring are not to be misinterpreted as brindling. *Black*–Blacks are all black. A black with brindle markings or a black with tan markings is a disqualification. *Yellow*–Yellows may range in color from fox-red to light cream, with variations in shading on the ears, back, and underparts of the dog. *Chocolate*–Chocolates can vary in shade from light to dark chocolate. Chocolate with brindle or tan markings is a disqualification.

Movement–Movement of the Labrador Retriever should be free and effortless. When watching a dog move toward oneself, there should be no sign of elbows out. Rather, the elbows should be held neatly to the body with the legs not too close together. Moving straight forward without pacing or weaving, the legs should form straight lines,

Permissible coat colors for the Lab are yellow, black, and chocolate.

Chocolate Labs

Like yellow, chocolate (liver) coloring has been present since the beginnings of the breed, and occurred in the St. Johns dogs from time to time. Liver is recessive to black, so it is possible to breed many generations without seeing a chocolate dog, especially since, again like yellows, many chocolate puppies were culled in the early days. Chocolates still suffer from prejudice in both the show ring and the hunt field, although they are gaining more acceptance all the time.

with all parts moving in the same plane. Upon viewing the dog from the rear, one should have the impression that the hind legs move as nearly as possible in a parallel line with the front legs. The hocks should do their full share of the work, flexing well, giving the appearance of power and strength. When viewed from the side, the shoulders should move freely and effortlessly, and the foreleg should reach forward close to the ground with extension. A short, choppy movement or high knee action indicates a straight shoulder; paddling indicates long, weak pasterns; and a short, stilted rear gait indicates a straight rear assembly; all are serious faults. Movement faults interfering with performance including weaving; side-winding; crossing over; high knee action; paddling; and short, choppy movement, should be severely penalized.

The ideal disposition for the Lab is one of a kindly, outgoing nature.

Temperament–True Labrador Retriever temperament is as much a hallmark of the breed as the "otter" tail. The ideal disposition is one of a kindly, outgoing, tractable nature; eager to please and non-aggressive towards man or animal. The Labrador has much that appeals to people; his gentle ways, intelligence and adaptability make him an ideal dog. Aggressiveness towards humans or other animals, or any evidence of shyness in an adult should be severely penalized.

Disqualifications

1. Any deviation from the height prescribed in the Standard.

2. A thoroughly pink nose or one lacking in any pigment.

3. Eye rims without pigment.

The Nose Knows

A "dudley" is a yellow Labrador Retriever with chocolate pigmentation—it has brown nose and eye rims rather than the correct black pigmentation. "Dudley" can also refer to a Lab of any color that has no pigmentation on the nose and eye rims, in which case they will be pink.

A lot of yellow Labs who have dark noses in the summer develop "snow nose" in the winter—the nose fades to pink. No one really knows why this happens, and it is not considered a fault. Come summer, the nose will darken again. To distinguish a snow nose from a dudley, check the color of the eye rims—a dudley will have pink or tan tissue, whereas a dog with snow nose but normal pigmentation will have black eye rims.

4. Docking or otherwise altering the length or natural carriage of the tail.

5. Any other color or a combination of colors other than black, yellow or chocolate as described in the Standard.

Approval Date: February 12, 1994

Effective Date: March 31, 1994

2

Finding Your Labrador Retriever

Examine a number of Labrador puppies before making your final selection.

Now you've done your homework, and you've decided that a Labrador Retriever is the dog for you. He'll suit your personality, lifestyle, and budget, and his good looks and happy, energetic demeanor appeal to you. Is it time to go out and get that Lab? No, sorry, not yet!

Before You Buy a Labrador Retriever

Individual Labrador Retrievers are not interchangeable. Although they share many traits, as in any family, there is variation among individuals. Let's look at some of the things you still need to think about before you get your Lab.

If you don't have the time to devote to a puppy, consider adopting an adult dog.

Puppy or Adult?

If you're like most people, when it's time to get a dog you think of a puppy. That's natural–after all, what's sweeter than a baby Lab? But a puppy really isn't the best choice for a lot of people, and that's especially true of Lab puppies. No question, baby Labs are about the cutest puppies going–but there's a lot more to owning one than puppy breath and photo opportunities. Puppies need lots of attention–they're babies, after all. They pee on carpets. They chew on things–and the wrong things can kill them. They're full or energy and enthusiasm, but they don't have much sense. The fat, round little puppy stage lasts only a few short weeks, and your little puppy turns into a rambunctious, long-legged adolescent, and stays that way for months–some Labs stay that way for years! If you want your Labrador Retriever puppy to emerge from adolescence as a well-mannered, happy adult, you need to spend lots of time (and patience) training, exercising, and socializing him during at least the first two to three years. If you and your family have the time, energy, and desire it takes to raise a puppy properly, then yours may be the right home for a carefully bred Lab pup. If not, please consider a mature dog instead.

Wonderful adult Labrador Retrievers are available for adoption, and really are a better option than a puppy for many people. Although some people think an older dog won't bond to a new owner, that's nonsense. Most adult adoptees bond just fine, and they make delightful companions. People also seem to worry that adopting an adult Lab means the sorrow of losing the dog that much sooner. No doubt, our canine companions live much too short a time. But the fact is that we can lose a dog at any age to accident or illness. I live right now with three dogs that came to me as adults, and they've been with me longer than one beautiful dog I got as a puppy and lost at four years of age. Besides, it's the quality of the time we spend with our friends that matters most.

So you think an adult Lab may fit into your life better than a young puppy–now where do you find one? There are at least three possibilities: a responsible breeder, a Lab rescue, or

Part 1

Did You Know?

Many people think that bitches—female dogs—make the best pets. Many Lab breeders suggest, though, that male Labrador Retrievers tend to be more dependent, sticking close to their people, while females tend to be more independent. Other Lab owners say that males are more prone to wandering if they get out of the house or fence. In the end, it really comes down to personal preference and the personality of the individual Lab. Males do tend to be a bit bigger and sometimes play more roughly than females, but they both make superb companions, especially when altered (spayed or castrated).

Older dogs bond to new homes just as well as puppies do.

a shelter. Breeders sometimes have older puppies and mature dogs to place in new homes. Sometimes a puppy just doesn't live up to its potential as a competitor or breeding dog. Sometimes a breeder has a retired show or breeding dog that would be happy to be someone's pet. Occasionally a dog is returned to its breeder because of some problem in its home–divorce, illness, or death, for instance–and is available for adoption. The advantage of adopting from a responsible breeder is that you should receive a complete history of the dog, including in many cases the results of health screening tests. While that is usually not true of Labs available through rescue and shelters, many of those are also super companions.

A Lab With a Purpose: Pet, Show, or Field Dog?

If you are looking for a pet–a canine companion whose full-time job is to be your pal–your best source is a responsible breeder of quality animals or a responsible rescue program. If you are looking for a dog for competition–conformation, obedience, agility, field trials, or

Is your dog going to be a show dog, field dog, or simply a family pet?

Buying from a responsible breeder will increase your chances of getting the best dog.

other sports–look for a breeder whose dogs have proven themselves successful in the sport (or sports) that interests you, or (for all but conformation) a rescued Lab fostered or evaluated by a rescuer who understands the sport. A person who is involved with your sport of interest will be more likely to have dogs with the talents you desire, and a knowledgeable breeder or rescuer understands the activity itself and will be better able to match you and the right puppy or dog. Within even a single litter, and more so within the breed, there is a wide range of personalities and potential. It's to your advantage to work with a breeder or rescuer who understands your vision of your Labrador Retriever.

Whatever your goals for your Labrador friend, remember that a poorly bred dog with physical or mental problems does not make a good competitor or hunter. If you buy from a breeder, please buy responsibly. If you adopt from a rescue or a shelter, be very clear with yourself and the people you contact about what you want–and do not want–in the dog you adopt.

Finding *Your* Labrador Retriever

Whether you decide on a puppy or an adult, male or female, please get your Lab from a responsible source. Remember, the Lab puppy you bring home is going to grow into a dog, and that dog will–hopefully–be with you for a long time. Let's look at the options.

Responsible Breeders

Responsible breeders are busy people. Most have several dogs to groom, train, exercise, and play with. Most breeders also have human families, jobs, and other obligations. Their breeding activities are conducted from their homes, not stores. Breeders are often gone on

A Responsible Breeder:

- Does not let puppies go to new homes until they are at least seven weeks old.
- Is happy to answer your questions—and is pleased that you are asking them!
- Welcomes you to visit and meet her and her dogs—with limitations while she has young puppies.
- Asks you as many questions as you ask her—she wants to know about your lifestyle, your family members, your experience with dogs, why you want a Lab, why you want one of her Labs, and lots more.
- Is a member of one or more breed clubs and/or training and performance clubs. Note: individuals cannot be "members" of the American Kennel Club (AKC)—if a breeder tells you she is, she is either ignorant of the facts or is intentionally misleading you.
- Breeds Labs that are at least two years old and that have cleared the recommended genetic screenings, and shows you the certificates.
- Has information on health clearances on most of the immediate relatives of the sire and dam, and shows you copies of the certificates or provides certificate numbers.
- Acknowledges that genetic problems do occur, and does not claim that her lines are free of health problems (no lines are completely free of health problems!).
- Offers a reasonable warrantee against inherited health and temperament problems or states specifically why she does not.
- Wants to know whether you plan to breed your dog, and is very cautious about selling you a breedable dog until you prove yourself responsible.
- Presents the negative aspects of owning a Lab.
- Socializes her puppies with people and other animals.
- Keeps her dogs in clean surroundings.
- Knows each dog by name, and knows each puppy as an individual.
- Provides references to previous buyers, and asks for your references.
- Sells only pups that are eligible for registration—she does not charge extra for "papers" and does not sell "purebred but unregistered" puppies. Sells pet puppies on Limited Registration.
- Does not pressure you to buy a puppy—on the contrary, she is very fussy about where her puppies go and makes you prove you're worthy!

weekends to participate with their dogs in various kinds of training or competition, so don't be offended if the breeder asks you to call again later, or doesn't return your call for a few days.

It's a good idea to have some questions ready when you call, but you can often learn a lot by letting someone simply talk. Listen carefully! I've been told complete nonsense by people who should know better. If you feel uneasy talking to a breeder, thank him for his time and go to the next name on your list. When you buy a puppy, you should be starting a long-term relationship with the breeder, not simply concluding a business transaction. The breeder should be a resource for you if you need advice or information, and should show an interest in what becomes of the puppy.

Now back to those questions. What should you ask? Start with general information. Find out how long the breeder has been in this breed and how many litters she has bred. If it's her first litter, that's not necessarily a bad thing–everyone starts somewhere, and some beginning breeders are well informed and very responsible. On the other hand, beware of a breeder that has bred several other breeds, jumped from one breed to another, or doesn't seem committed to breeding good quality dogs. Beware also the breeder, big or small, who tells you things your research tells you are wrong. I recently had a well-known breeder tell me that all orthopedic problems are caused by owners after they take their puppies home. That's nonsense, of course, and that's not a breeder I would want to deal with.

Ask lots of questions when talking to the breeder and be prepared to answer a few, as well.

Ask the breeder what his goals are. Is he trying to produce winning conformation dogs, or athletic, highly trainable Labs that will excel in fieldwork, obedience, or agility? Does he breed to produce the kind of Lab developed and prized by hunters? Does he want to produce versatile Labs that can perform in several arenas? A breeder's goals, and his success at meeting them, affect whether he's likely to have the sort of Lab you want. If the breeder doesn't seem to have any goals except to have some puppies and make some money, look for someone else.

Ask about the breeder's dogs' bloodlines. Even if you don't know anything about the dogs mentioned in various pedigrees, the answer will tell you about the breeder. Serious breeders know their dogs' bloodlines well and can recite pedigrees from memory. If the breeder doesn't seem to know the canine family tree, chances are she's not serious about producing high-quality dogs.

A pup that hides whenever approached probably won't make the best family pet.

But wait–you just want a pet, so why bother with all this stuff? Careful breeding is the key to fine companions–and what better position could a Labrador Retriever aspire to than to be someone's best friend? But producing fine companions is not so easy, and involves a lot more than mating any two dogs. Even in a carefully planned litter from accomplished parents and grandparents, there will be puppies that just aren't cut out for competition. Often the "fault" is so minor that most people won't see it even if the breeder points it out. Such "pet" puppies from a high-quality litter will be healthier and closer to the breed standard in looks and disposition than the best puppy from a poor quality breeding. And a responsible breeder will do everything possible to find your puppy in the litter–the one with the personality traits best suited to your needs.

Responsible breeders nearly always offer and require a written contract, which should be designed to protect you, the breeder, and the puppy. You should have an opportunity to read the contract before you commit to purchasing the puppy, preferably at least a few days before you're scheduled to pick up your puppy. If a guarantee is offered, the terms should be clearly stated in the purchase contract. The contract should state anything you are required to do, such as spay or neuter your puppy, feed a certain food, keep the puppy as a house dog, or whatever. It should also specify what the breeder's obligations to you are, and it should include terms for return of the puppy if that becomes necessary. My best advice is this: *don't forego a written contract.* I've done that a few times and have lived to regret it. If you're not comfortable with the terms or the terms are vague or incomplete, ask the breeder to change them or state them more clearly–or look for another breeder.

Ask to see the puppy's health records to ensure that he is indeed healthy.

Health Guarantees

Most of the advice you'll read on how to buy a puppy will tell you to buy only from breeders who guarantee their puppies against inherited diseases for several years or even for life. Realistically, though, no one can guarantee that a puppy (or any living thing) will have no health problems. Most genetic diseases are complex in nature, and some are very difficult to eradicate. The best a breeder can do is to screen all dogs that are active in the breeding program, obtain information about the screening of as many relatives as possible, and breed carefully based on that information. Since dogs are not interchangeable like most other things we buy with guarantees, and since there are emotional and ethical issues not involved with cars and refrigerators, it's important that puppy buyers understand what a health guarantee is and isn't. So what *is* a "health guarantee" on a Labrador Retriever puppy?

Your breeder should, of course, guarantee absolutely that your puppy is healthy when you take him home. Such guarantees usually cover the first 48 to 72 hours–enough time for you to get your pup to your veterinarian for a checkup, but not so much time that your pup will be likely to contract a disease after leaving the breeder. (Remember–your puppy will not be well protected against disease until he's about four months old and has completed his puppy shots, so you need to protect him as far as possible from exposure to infection.)

Your breeder should also offer a written guarantee or warranty against the major genetic diseases found in Labrador Retrievers, particularly hip and elbow dysplasia, or should explain why such a guarantee is not offered. Some breeders offer to replace affected puppies. If that's the case, be certain you understand the terms. Will you have to give back the first puppy? Will you have to take the second puppy within a certain time frame? Will the second puppy be from the same parent or parents or be closely related to the first pup? A few breeders offer financial compensation instead of a replacement puppy, but that's rare. I know some responsible breeders who screen carefully and breed carefully, but feel they should not be held responsible for problems they cannot realistically prevent if they inform their puppy buyers of the risk. Only you can decide whether you are comfortable with the breeder's position, whatever it is.

You should take your new Lab pup to the vet for a checkup within the first 48 to 72 hours.

How to Find a Responsible Breeder

How do you find one of these responsible breeders? Start with your local kennel club or Lab club. The American Kennel Club (AKC) and the Labrador Retriever Club (LRC) can direct you to the club or clubs nearest to you. Keep in mind, though, that the lists they provide are just leads–you still need to check out each breeder you decide to contact.

The newspaper may lead you to a well-bred puppy, but if you respond to newspaper ads, be cautious, ask questions, and be prepared to walk away without a puppy if the breeder and dogs don't measure up. Most established breeders don't need to advertise in the newspaper because they have a waiting list for their puppies. Dog magazines also list breeders, but some very nice ads are placed by puppy mill operations. If a breeder always has puppies available or on the way, beware!

Once you've decided that a Lab is for you, you need to find the right breeder.

Referrals are an excellent way to find a puppy. If you see a Lab you like, find out where it came from. Find out if the owner is happy with the dog, and if she would go back to the same breeder for another pup. Even if that breeder doesn't have a puppy for you, she can probably refer you to people with good dogs from the same or similar bloodlines.

Searching on the Internet may turn up the right Lab for You.

Dog shows can also be a good place to meet breeders, and to see lots of dogs. You won't find puppies for sale–that is against AKC rules–but you will see lots of dogs, some local and some from far afield. Please remember that the breeders you see are preparing their dogs for competition and are often busy and stressed. They shouldn't be downright rude to you, but please don't expect people to stop to talk to you, especially before their dogs go into the ring. Buy a catalog, find a seat, and enjoy the show! Many people are more relaxed after their dogs have shown, or you can contact them later. Ask for business cards where appropriate, or mark the names of breeders whose dogs you like in your catalog, and look up their phone numbers later.

The Internet is also a good puppy-search tool, if you proceed cautiously. Labrador Retriever discussion lists and bulletin boards can lead you to breeders, and give you a chance to size them up from what they write. (It's amazing how much you can learn about people just by watching what they post over a few weeks!) Websites, too, can give you lots of information, but they can also be misleading. Verify all claims made on websites or elsewhere. It's also a good idea to look for people who have purchased puppies or dogs from the breeder and to ask what their experiences have been. In this electronic age, you can often locate a breeder's puppy buyers through Internet discussion lists, bulletin boards, and searches using the breeder's name or kennel name.

Contact a few promising breeders by telephone or Internet first. When you've narrowed your choices down to two or three, arrange to visit each one if possible. Don't visit them one right after another, though, particularly if they have puppies at the time. It's very easy to transmit disease from one place to another. Go home, shower, and change clothes, including your shoes, between visits.

When you visit, don't focus completely on cute puppies! (I know, it's hard to think rationally when looking at roly-poly Labrador babies, but it's important.) Are the facilities clean? Do the dogs seem to be healthy, reasonably clean, and well groomed? Do they have access to clean water, and room to move around and play? Are the dogs friendly? Does the breeder know every one of them by name? The answers to all these questions should be yes.

When visiting a breeder, you should be able to meet the dam, and the sire if he's present.

You should be able to meet the mother unless the puppies are very young. Don't expect her to look her best while she's nursing, but do pay attention to her temperament. Most Lab bitches are friendly even when they have pups as long as someone they know and trust is present. If the sire is present, you should be able to meet him as well. Serious breeders often breed their bitches to stud dogs owned by other people, though, so the sire may not be available. The breeder should have pictures of him and copies of his health clearances, title certificates, registration, and other important paperwork. She should be able to tell you about him, and why she chose him for this bitch. Ask also if there are other relatives available for you to meet. If there are, you'll get a better idea of the looks and temperaments of the whole family. If you don't like what you see, don't buy the puppy!

The breeder should give you copies of the paperwork pertinent to the litter *before* you commit to the purchase. Pedigrees, registration papers, and health clearances are not proprietary information, and a good breeder will be proud to show you how good the dogs "look on paper." The breeder should show you the parents' registration papers and the individual registration applications for the puppies or a copy of the litter registration if the individual applications aren't back from AKC yet. Be aware, though, that registration with the AKC or other registries does not indicate quality in the breeding dogs or the puppies. It merely shows that the parents of the puppies are registered, and that they are purebred as far as the registry knows.

The breeder should give you a copy of the litter's pedigree, or family tree, showing three to five generations. Look for initials indicating titles earned in competition–for instance, "Ch." means "Champion." At least a third to a half the dogs in the first two generations (the puppies' parents and grandparents) should have titles. Ask the breeder if any of them are "pointed," meaning that they have some of the points needed to complete the championship. It's very difficult to finish a championship on a Lab because so many are in competition, but there should still be some evidence that the breeder takes quality seriously enough to compete in one or more areas of competition. Many carelessly bred puppies are advertised as having "champion bloodlines" and there may indeed be a champion or two several generations back. But the parents and grandparents have the most influence on the traits in the puppies, and you have no way to assess the quality of untitled dogs unless you can see them, and you have the knowledge to evaluate them.

The breeder should show you the appropriate certification showing that the parents have been tested and certified free of genetic disease. At a minimum, Lab parents and grandparents should be certified free of hip and elbow dysplasia, and many breeders also have their dogs tested for thyroid function and healthy hearts and eyes. Even better, the parents' siblings and older offspring should be certified. Don't take anyone's word for the testing–I made that mistake and a few months later had huge vet bills for surgery on my Lab's elbows. It turned out her mother had not been certified (although the breeder told me she had), and that both her parents had produced other puppies with elbow and hip problems.

The breeder should ask you to sign a contract when you purchase your pup.

Now the question that's probably been on your mind–how much? Of course, price is important, but don't sacrifice quality to price–you'll get no bargain doing that! In the long run you are better off paying more for a puppy that has been carefully bred and raised, and that is backed by a good contract and a responsible breeder, than you are paying less for a lesser quality pup. Prices vary around the country, but you should expect to pay about $500 to $800 for a Lab pup from a reputable breeder. Consider this: if you pay $500 for a puppy, and it lives to be 10 years old, you've spent $50 a year–that's less than a dollar a week for a best friend and playmate! Isn't it worth a little more to increase the chances that your Lab will be healthy in mind and body?

Most responsible breeders use written contracts designed to protect the breeder, the buyer, and especially the puppy. A good contract is written clearly and covers several concerns. First, health guarantees, which we touched on earlier. You should have at least 48 hours to have the puppy examined by a veterinarian and to return the puppy for a full refund if the vet finds that it is not healthy. The contract should also cover inherited diseases. No one can guarantee that a puppy won't inherit a health problem, but many breeders offer compensation if that happens. If the breeder does not offer such compensation, be sure you understand why not, and be sure that you are satisfied with the terms of the guarantee. If you're not, and the breeder won't negotiate, then look somewhere else for your puppy.

If you're buying a pet, expect to see a clause requiring you to have the dog spayed or neutered and prohibiting you from breeding it. Breeders who are committed to the welfare of Labrador Retrievers as a breed use such terms to help keep puppies out of the hands of irresponsible breeders. It may also be that the puppy you are buying has a fault that the breeder feels should not be reproduced. If you want to breed your Lab eventually, be honest about that. Find a breeder who will work with you as a mentor, buy a breeding-quality dog, and do it right.

A responsible breeder will accept back any dog she sells you at any time in its life. In fact, many breeders require that you give them the opportunity to take the dog before you try to place it anywhere else. Naturally, breeders prefer to place each puppy in a good lifelong home, but they also understand that life isn't always what we expect, and they care what happens to every puppy for its entire life. That's why good breeders ask you lots of questions before agreeing to sell you a puppy. If a breeder doesn't want to know anything about where and how her puppy will live, how much do you think she'll care about your satisfaction as a puppy owner?

Choosing Your Puppy

Once you have found a breeder with dogs you like, you may have to wait a while for a litter and a puppy to become available. Be patient–this is a good time to read everything you can about Labs, and dogs in general, and dog training. The more you understand your future dog, the more you'll enjoy him throughout his life.

Eventually the time will come to pick your special puppy. Trust me, you're going to get all sorts of advice on how to do it! Some people will tell you to let the puppy choose you.

Ask to examine the puppy away from his littermates to make sure that he is the one for you.

That works out sometimes, but the pushy pup who climbs on everyone and shoves his littermates out of the way may be a more dominant adult than you care to live with. And if you visit the puppies only once or twice, which is all most buyers can do, your knowledge of the individuals in the litter will be limited.

Other people recommend "testing" the pups. Temperament and aptitude testing will give you some idea of a puppy's personality, but there's no evidence that these tests are accurate in predicting the adult personality. Young puppies are often more submissive than they will be as adults, and adolescent dogs–like human teenagers–are often pushier than they will be as adults. A Labrador Retriever puppy should be playful, friendly, and alert. He should be interested in people and in his littermates and other animals. *Do not* buy a shy Lab puppy, or one that appears to be aggressive with his littermates or people.

Adopting a Lab from a rescue organization may be an option.

The best way to choose a puppy from a responsible breeder is to let the breeder make the match. Tell the breeder what you want–and do not want–in a dog, and what you plan to do with the dog, and let her choose or help you choose the right pup. Good breeders observe their puppies for hours every day, and they know the individuals very well.

Remember, too, that when you take home a seven- to ten-week-old pup, no matter how well bred he is, you take potential. The rest is up to you. You need to train and socialize that puppy, and give him proper nutrition, exercise, and health care if he is to fulfill his promise.

Rescued Labs as Pets

Unfortunately, some Labs find themselves the unwitting victims of the breed's many virtues. The fact is that *no*

Characteristics of a Healthy Lab Puppy (7 to 12 weeks old)

- A healthy puppy is solid and well proportioned.
- A healthy puppy is not excessively thin (ribs should not be visible on a baby puppy—a skinny puppy may be malnourished or ill).
- A healthy puppy is not pot-bellied (a healthy chubby puppy is one thing—a thin pup with a pot-belly may be infested with roundworms).
- A healthy puppy's fur is soft and glossy.
- A healthy puppy is free of fleas. To check, gently push fur against the direction of growth—black specks at the skin may be "flea dirt."
- A healthy puppy has healthy skin. It has no red, itchy spots or bald or scaly patches.
- A healthy puppy has a clean rectal area. Small white matter resembling grains of rice around the anus may be tapeworm segments, indicating that the puppy has intestinal tapeworm and has or has had fleas (tapeworm is most often acquired when the pup ingests an infected flea). Signs of diarrhea may indicate that the puppy is ill.
- A healthy puppy has bright, clear eyes that follow movement. There should be no crusting or redness on the eyelids. The third eyelid (in the inner corner each eye) should not be visible when the puppy is awake.
- A healthy puppy has pink gums, and healthy breath smelling only of the slightly musky odor of "puppy breath." His jaws appear to aligned with one another, and he does not appear to have an underbite or big overbite, any of which can interfere with proper chewing.
- A healthy puppy has a slightly damp but clean nose, with no fresh or crusted discharge. He breathes normally, without sneezing, coughing, or wheezing.
- A healthy puppy has clean ears, free of odor, inflammation, dirty-looking buildup, or discharge. He does not shake his head or scratch at his ears a lot.
- A healthy puppy moves freely with no signs of lameness.
- A healthy Lab puppy is happy and lively—unless he's asleep!

breed of dog–not even America's most popular–is appropriate for every dog owner. Unfortunately for some dogs, and their owners, many people don't do enough research before they get a Lab and realize too late that they really can't manage such a big, active dog. Other Labs find themselves in need due to their owners' death or serious illness. And some Labs wander off and never find their way home. Lab rescue is there for such dogs, and others, in need of homes.

What Is Lab Rescue?

"Rescue" refers to individuals and groups who take in, foster, and place dogs or other animals in suitable new homes. As part of this widespread purebred rescue system, Lab rescuers help Labs that need new homes for all sorts of reasons. Rescuers are nearly always unpaid volunteers who donate their time, dog-handling skills, and love.

From what do Labs need to be rescued? Sometimes tragedy disrupts a dog's home–perhaps death or disablement of the owner, or a serious change in personal or family circumstances. Other Labs are found as strays and cannot be returned to their owners. Legal action against a puppy mill or other business or individual sometimes results in confiscation of Labs, and rescuers step in to help find them new homes. Occasionally a dog is abandoned at a veterinary office, boarding kennel, or groomer. Very often Labrador Retrievers wind up in rescue because their first owners chose the breed without doing careful research first and then found that an untrained, rambunctious, big young dog was just too much to handle. Rather than put in the time and work to teach the dog what it needs to know, they turn it over to rescue. Sometimes nothing is known about a dog's background–perhaps it was a stray or was dropped at a shelter with no information.

National Labrador Rescue Information

The Labrador Retriever Club offers rescue support for those interested in adopting a rescue Lab. Contact the National Coordinator through the LRC's website at `http://thelabradorclub.com/rescue`.

Although puppies are occasionally available through rescue programs, most rescued Labs are older adolescents or adults. Some have behavioral problems due to insufficient exercise, training, and socialization, but many do not. Many rescued Labs were probably purchased as puppies by people who failed to do what is necessary to raise a Lab properly–they may have thought that love is enough, but it's not.

Most rescued dogs spend some time in a volunteer foster home before they are placed in new homes. Fostering allows rescuers to evaluate the dog's temperament, behavior, and training status in a "normal" environment, which is much better than a kennel environment provides. Foster caretakers can identify a dog's individual strengths and needs, which is important when matching a dog to a new home. If a rescued dog is sexually intact, it is spayed or neutered before it is placed, or within a limited time after placement. Because many Labs enter rescue in need of training, rescuers try to provide basic obedience and house manners training. The basic health status of each rescued animal is checked, and although rescue programs usually can't afford to do everything that every dog needs, the new owners can be informed about possible problems.

Adopting a Rescued Lab

Good Lab rescuers try very hard to match each rescued Lab with the right Lab lover. As a potential adopter, you will submit a detailed application form, provide references, and agree to a home visit by a rescue volunteer. After you are approved, rescue volunteers will try to match you with a dog that needs a home. If you decide to adopt, be patient–it may take several weeks or even months to find the right dog. But good things are worth the wait!

Adoption fees vary from under a hundred to several hundred dollars, depending on the dog's age, health status, veterinary care needed prior to placement (including spaying or neutering), the particular rescue group's resources and policies, and other factors. Many groups have not-for-profit status, and ask for a donation rather than a fee, and the donation is tax deductible.

When the right dog is found for you, you'll be required to sign an adoption agreement. You should be given general information about Labs and specific information about your new buddy. Your rescue representative should be willing to answer questions even after you take your dog home, and *all* rescuers love to hear from their former charges and to get pictures from time to time. That's how they know that all their time, money, and emotion is well spent.

Purebred Labs are sometimes available from shelters.

Shelters

Sometimes good Labrador Retrievers can be found in animal shelters and pounds. Some are brought in by their owners for the same reasons as some are given to rescue groups. Others are picked up as strays and never claimed by their owners.

If it's important to you that the dog you adopt really is a Lab or a Lab cross or mix, and if you don't feel competent to make that call on your own, then take someone with you who really knows Labrador Retrievers to help evaluate candidates. Some shelter workers are very knowledgeable about dogs; some are not. I was called once to pick up a "Lab" from our local shelter. When I got there, the dog in the kennel they directed me to was a black dog, about 35 pounds and fluffy coated. Two kennels down from it was a gorgeous, obviously (to me) purebred black Lab. The person who called me didn't think he was a Lab, but thought the other was. All too many black dogs are labeled "Lab" or "Lab mix" when in fact they may have little or no Labrador Retriever in them at all. A dog doesn't have to be a Lab to be a great pet, but if you want to be reasonably sure of getting a true Lab temperament, it will pay to go slowly and carefully when adopting a shelter dog.

3

Welcoming Your Lab

Bringing Your Puppy Home

An old wive's tale has it that if you don't bring your puppy home at exactly seven weeks of age, it will never bond to you and your family. Nonsense! Forty-nine days–seven weeks–is certainly the youngest a puppy should leave its littermates and mama, but it's not necessarily the best time. Puppies learn faster between seven and eight weeks of age than at any other time in their lives, so if you have time to spend teaching your puppy–during short, positive training sessions–you can accomplish a lot in this one week. If you can't devote a lot of time to the pup, then it may be better to wait a couple more weeks to bring him home. You will again want to ask the breeder how she handles puppies during

Lab pups learn a lot from seven to ten weeks of age.

Labs are born water dogs.

this critical period. She should spend time with each pup and begin potty training, and also begin to separate the pups into smaller groups, and let each one spend some time away from his littermates. Puppies at this age can learn simple commands, including sit, down, stand, and come, and can learn to walk quietly on a leash. If you want a well-adjusted pup, do *not* purchase one that has been isolated from human contact during this critical socialization period!

From eight to ten weeks of age, puppies go through their first fear imprint period–which is another important consideration when deciding when to take your puppy home. During this time, traumatic events can have long-lasting effects, so pups should not be exposed to potentially frightening or painful experiences.

Puppy-proofing your home and yard can be a challenge.

Puppy-Proofing Your Home

Puppies chew. They chew whatever they can grab. Your puppy doesn't know the difference between your good shoes, your child's favorite toy, and the Nylabone® you gave him. Expecting him to make that distinction is like asking a toddler to play with his ball but not to touch the vase on the coffee table. It's your responsibility to protect both your puppy and your possessions.

There is really only one way to keep your puppy safe from household and garden dangers and to keep your possessions safe from your puppy: prevention. Remove temptations from easy reach and confine your puppy to a safe area when you can't supervise him until he his old enough to be trustworthy (which varies with Lab pups from six months to two years or older). Do this even if you're adopting an older puppy or an adult. Even if the dog hasn't chewed anything up in years in his old

Puppy-Proofing Hints

1. Place all breakables out of reach.
2. Place all hazards, especially small things that a puppy may swallow, out of reach—for instance, pin cushions and boxes, needles and thread, coins, metal objects, small toys...anything a puppy might eat, even if you wouldn't!
3. Shield all electrical and telephone cords from puppy teeth.
4. Never leave a puppy unsupervised where he could get into trouble.

home, the stress of a new environment may cause him to seek relief in chewing things.

Puppy-proofing your home is much like childproofing. Put all breakables out of reach and make sure that hazards are inaccessible. Keep in mind that puppies are smaller and more active than toddlers are and can crawl under, through, over, and around things that babies can't. And although babies do shove all sorts of things into their little mouths, puppies have sharper teeth and a stronger urge to bite and chew.

Get down on your hands and knees and look at things from puppy level. Protect electrical and telephone wires–you can purchase specially designed sheaths for them, or make your own with PVC pipe. Remove potential dangers like pin boxes and pin cushions, razor blades, tobacco products, chocolate, and so on from reach–that includes waste baskets and the edge of the bathtub. Puppies have been known to die from ingesting the unthinkable, and Lab puppies are especially interested in putting things in their mouths. After all, their ancestors were bred to carry things! Puppies can be great at teaching children to put toys away, but ingesting little toy soldiers and Barbie doll heads isn't very good for puppy's health, so if you have children, be diligent in encouraging them to keep things picked up "so the puppy doesn't get hurt" (a much better motivator than neatness alone!).

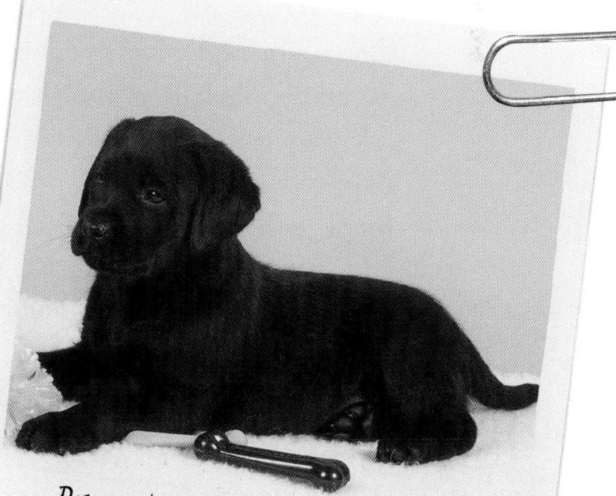

Provide your Lab with safe chew toys, such as those made by Nylabone®.

The Nylabone® Fold-Away Pet Carrier is the ideal crate for your Lab.

You can also begin right away to teach your pup what is legal to chew. If he picks up something he shouldn't, gently take it away and replace it with one of his toys. Always supply your dog with safe chew toys, such as those made by Nylabone®. There's no need to yell, and certainly no need for physical punishment. Just teach him gently, and he'll get the idea.

There are lots of products on the market that are supposed to keep puppies from chewing, and many people also recommend such household products as hot sauce, hot mustard, and lemon juice. These may work on some pups, but in my experience Labrador puppies regard them as condiments, thank you very much. I once bought some "dog repellant" to fasten to my garden plants with twisty ties. I spent half an hour fastening the silly things to shrubs in my back yard only to discover that my Lab pup, Raja, was following me and eating them! Supervision and training are your best bet.

Get Your Lab a Crate

One of the best ways to control your puppy when you cannot supervise him is with a crate. Some people balk at the idea of crating a dog. But before you decide that a crate is cruel, ask yourself this: would you turn a preschooler loose unsupervised in your house? Your puppy is a canine child, prone to explore, to put things in its mouth, and to potty when the urge hits, unaware of what's "right" and "wrong," safe and unsafe.

Used properly, a crate will keep your puppy–and your belongings–safe. Since you will supervise free time, your pup will learn what is allowed and what is not. Besides, housetraining is easier with a crate (more on that in Chapter 6). Healthy dogs raised in clean environments are naturally inclined to keep their sleeping areas clean, so crating a puppy for reasonable lengths of time encourages housetraining.

Hazards Around Your Home

A safe and welcoming environment–that's what home should be for our dogs and ourselves. But it's important to recognize that our homes also harbor many hazards for active puppies and dogs, and it's up to us to keep our pets as safe as possible. Some simple precautions will go a long way to protecting your Lab from dangers on the home front.

Certain plants can be fatal to your puppy. Keep an eye on him when he's outside.

Garden Hazards

Hundreds of common garden and house plants are known to be poisonous to pets, including azaleas and rhododendron, daffodils, larkspur, philodendrons, Dieffenbachia, tomato plant leaves, and many others. The toxins in plants can affect a dog's cardiovascular, gastrointestinal, and neurological systems. If you garden or keep houseplants, ask your veterinarian or your local agricultural service for a list of plants that may be dangerous to your dog.

Garden chemicals, including fertilizers, herbicides, and insecticides, are also dangerous to dogs. Most Labs will eat nearly anything, and mine have all enjoyed nibbling on grass and other plants and fruits. If you have your lawn sprayed or you use chemicals on your garden, your pup may be accidentally poisoned. Be sure to observe any recommended period for keeping pets away from the treated area. If your neighbors treat their yards, use caution as well, since the wind can carry toxins from their treatment onto your grass and plants. Beware, too, of letting your dog swim in water that may have chemicals from run off, such as ponds surrounded by beautiful lawns. I know a dog that nearly died from exposure to herbicides in a golf course pond. If you used slug bait, ant poisons, or mouse or rat poisons, be sure that they are completely inaccessible to your puppy. Remember, they are made to taste good to attract their intended victims, but they will also attract your dog.

> **If You Think Your Lab's Been Poisoned**
>
> The National Animal Poison Control Center (NAPCC) is available 24 hours a day at 1-888-426-4435 or at 1-900-680-0000. For more information on the NAPCC, contact their website at *www.napcc.aspca.org.*

Symptoms of poisoning include vomiting, diarrhea, loss of appetite, swelling of the tongue and other mouth

Part 1

Protecting Your Pup from Household and Garden Poisons

- Keep your puppy out of vegetable and flower gardens, and compost.
- Keep houseplants out of reach of your puppy.
- Follow directions for drying times on all lawn treatments.
- Be sure slug bait, insecticides, and rodenticides are out of your puppy's reach.
- Dispose of containers for hazardous products where your pup can't get them.
- Store antifreeze and other poisons in tightly sealed containers out of reach of a curious puppy.

tissues, excessive salivation, or seizures. If your dog displays these symptoms, or if you know or suspect that he's ingested something poisonous, get him to the vet as quickly as possible. If he has no symptoms, or has symptoms that go away, take him to the vet anyway. Some poisons take a while to show their effect, and by then it may be too late. Your dog's life may depend on your response time. If possible, take a sample of whatever he's ingested to your vet–a leaf from the plant (or the plant's scientific name, if you know it) or container for a chemical or medication.

Some creatures common to our gardens can also be hazardous. Dogs, like people, can be allergic to bee stings–and to complicate matters, many dogs snap at the buzzing. I had a Lab who liked to eat bees for the sweet nectar they carried. Fortunately he wasn't allergic, because he did get stung occasionally–apparently he thought the reward was worth the pain. Spiders are also poisonous, some more than others, and in some parts of the country, scorpions and other creatures may be a threat. If you notice your puppy swelling up around the face or elsewhere, get him to the vet–with the beast that bit or stung him if possible.

Bug bites can be just as annoying to your dog as they are to you.

Anti-freeze

Anti-freeze (*ethylene glycol*) is lethal. Unfortunately, it also smells and tastes sweet, and pets will lap it up. Five tablespoons full of antifreeze can kill a thirty-pound puppy. If you notice antifreeze leaking from your car's radiator, have the hoses and connectors checked, and thoroughly clean the area where the drip occurred. Don't leave pans of antifreeze sitting around where your pets might get into them, even for a few minutes. If your pup does ingest antifreeze, or you even think he may have, get him to a veterinarian *immediately*. Don't wait for symptoms to appear–by that time he will likely have permanent and possibly fatal kidney damage.

The First Few Nights

It's natural for your puppy to cry during the first few nights in his new home. He's used to sleeping, playing, and eating with his brothers and sisters, and probably his dam as well. He wants to stay with the pack at night. Remember, dogs are social animals–they live together, eat together, play together, and sleep together. Puppies sleep tangled up with their siblings. Now your new pup is in a strange place with a strange pack, and he may well cry for company and reassurance.

Labs bond very closely with their people and will begin this bonding process very quickly.

Labrador Retrievers bond very closely with their people, and even young puppies will begin this bonding process very quickly. If possible, put your puppy's crate in your bedroom at night. Your puppy will feel more secure if he can hear you and smell you close by. You'll also hear him stirring in the middle of the night, and will be able to hustle him outside to potty, which will speed up housetraining. If your puppy whines in his crate, and you're certain he doesn't need to potty, ignore him. That may be tough the first night or two, but if you can stand it he'll quickly learn that whining and yapping get him nowhere, and he'll quiet down. If he keeps it up for more than about five minutes, slap the top of the crate once, and say, "Quiet," in a moderate voice. Don't shout. You might give him a chew toy (although a Nylabone® at night works something like a drum in the hands of a three-year-old child!). The goal is to teach your puppy that he is safe–you are right there–but it's time to sleep. Remember, though, that he's a baby, and be patient. Do you know a baby who didn't give his parents a few wakeful nights? If your puppy absolutely cannot sleep in your bedroom, put an old sweatshirt with your scent on it in his crate, place a ticking clock or a radio set low nearby to make him feel less alone and to sooth him. But you should expect some crying the first few nights.

Provide your pup with a comfortable, safe place to sleep.

You can make things a bit easier by preparing your puppy for bedtime. If you let him sleep all evening, he'll be well rested and ready to play when you're ready to hit the sack! Instead, play with him, brush him, and encourage him to play with his toys during the evening. Give him a vigorous playtime followed by a potty trip just before bedtime. Tired puppies are good puppies.

A Safe and Comfortable Environment

Labrador Retrievers are, overall, very hardy and adaptable dogs. Give him his daily food, regular health care, lots of exercise, plenty of affection, training for proper manners, and a warm, dry place to sleep (preferably where he can hear you and smell you through his dreams), and you'll have a happy dog. You'll also have a safer dog than one that lives outside.

Most pet Labs are housedogs. I can't think of anything lovelier than the sight of a Labrador Retriever sleeping contentedly through the evening near his human family–or on the couch with his head in someone's lap! If you take the time to train your Lab, he'll be trustworthy and I think you'll find his companionship well worth the extra vacuuming. If you must keep your Lab outdoors, please give him a proper living environment, companionship, and daily attention.

Proper Shelter and Care

Many Labs do live happily in kennel environments. This is particularly true of Labs belonging to breeders and hunters who have quite a few dogs–too many to feel comfortable in the house. Labs that have good, clean, dry living quarters and that have lots of daily activity and the companionship of dogs and people live good lives. A healthy, properly conditioned Labrador Retriever can tolerate a wide range of environmental conditions, which is one of the things that makes the breed attractive. But overall, I'm not keen on keeping companion dogs outdoors full time, especially alone.

Your Lab wants nothing more than to be by your side, day and night. If you have only one dog, please do not banish him to a solitary life without companionship. He's a social animal and he needs companionship to remain emotionally healthy. He needs mental and physical exercise for his mind and body. He needs someone to play with for his soul.

Please don't keep your Lab outdoors unless you can give him daily attention. That doesn't mean just giving him food and water. He needs to be with you for several hours *every day*, playing or working. It's your responsibility to see that he gets proper exercise and to check his physical condition every day. Aside from daily attention and care, your Lab needs and deserves to live in decent conditions.

If you have to leave your Lab outdoors, make sure he is in a fenced-in area.

Your dog needs proper shelter with clean bedding year round. When it's warm out, he needs well-ventilated shade. When it's cold, he needs a properly insulated doghouse or other shelter of the right size. We may crave big houses, but an oversize doghouse does your dog no good in winter. He should have just enough room to lie down comfortably. If the house is bigger than that, it won't keep your dog warm, and in severe weather, he could suffer hypothermia and frostbite.

Provide your dog with fresh water when he's outside.

Your dog needs access to fresh, clean water year round. In the summer, the water bowl should be cleaned often to prevent the growth of bacteria and algae, and it should be freshened at least twice a day. In winter, your dog needs water at all times–ice and snow are not sufficient. Use a heated bucket or bowls with a metal-wrapped chew-safe cord designed for use with animals. Heated bowls are available from pet supply and farm stores. Avoid metal bowls, which freeze quickly, and plastic or ceramic bowls, which crack when the water freezes.

Your outdoor dog needs proper portions of good-quality food. He should be fed regular meals, and his food bowls should be picked up and washed after every meal. Any bits of food or spillage should also be cleaned up. Food left out can go bad and make your dog ill if he eats it later, and leftovers will encourage rodents, insects, and bacteria. In cold weather, an outdoor dog will need one-quarter to one-third more food than he needs in warm weather in order to generate enough body heat.

If your Lab must live outdoors, you still need to provide him with all the routine care of an indoor dog–training, grooming, play, and outings that give him variety and stimulation. Your dog needs regular veterinary care and proper health maintenance at home. Above all, he needs to know that you love him, and he needs the chance to love you back. Don't get a dog if he'll live alone and lonely.

In hot weather, it is best to exercise your Lab early or late in the day when it is cool out.

Keeping Your Lab Safe in Warm Weather

Labs and Lab owners alike have all sorts of outdoor fun in warm weather, but heat and sun can also be dangerous for your dog. One very real hazard for Labs is hyperthermia, or overheating. Because he doesn't sweat except through the pads of his feet, your dog can't cool his body as easily as you can. If his body temperature rises and stays above normal for very long, he can die. Black and chocolate Labs are especially prone to overheating because their dark coats absorb heat. But there are some things you can do to prevent overheating.

Exercise your dog early in the morning or in the evening when it's cooler than the middle of the day. Be particularly careful when the humidity is high–it makes it harder for your dog to cool off. If you plan to have him out in the heat for more than 20 minutes, carry cool water for both of you and offer it about every 20 minutes. Lightweight portable water dishes are available for carrying on walks. Try to walk in the shade, and watch for signs of overheating. If necessary, stop and rest in a shady spot and let your dog cool off a bit before heading home. You can also cool your dog by wetting his belly, earflaps, and the pads of his feet with cool water. Don't wet the whole dog unless he can lie down in a shady spot–exercising when wet on a hot day will turn your Lab into his own sauna and actually raise his body temperature.

Prevent Heatstroke

Heatstroke can kill your Lab very quickly. Never leave your dog in a car on a warm day, even for a few minutes. Don't leave him outside on concrete or asphalt or without shade. Make sure he has constant access to cool, clean water. Don't exercise him during the heat of the day. Keep your Lab indoors and cool if he has trouble breathing, is overweight, has a history of heatstroke, is ill, or is elderly.

If your dog is active in hot weather, watch for symptoms of heatstroke, which include some or all of the following: pale or bright red gums; bright red tongue; thick, sticky saliva; rapid panting; vomiting; diarrhea; apparent dizziness or weakness; shock. If your Lab has any of these symptoms, take his temperature if possible. A dog with moderate heatstroke (body temperature from 104°F-106°F) will probably recover if given first aid immediately. Use a hose, shower, or tub of cold water to wet and cool him. Check his temperature every 10 minutes and continue the cooling process until his temperature is down to 103°F. Give him a rehydration fluid (such as a sports drink) or water, and get him to a veterinarian.

Severe heatstroke (body temperature over 106°F) can cause death or permanent damage. If your dog's temperature is 106°F or higher, he needs immediate first aid and veterinary treatment. If you're more than five minutes from the vet and your dog is conscious, follow the cooling procedures outlined above until his temperature is down to 106°F, then wrap him in a cool wet towel or blanket and proceed to the vet. If you can get him to the vet in fewer than five minutes, or if he's unconscious, just wrap him in a cool wet towel or blanket, and go to the vet. If you need to take your dog to a veterinarian in an emergency, call before you leave, or have someone call for you. That will allow the vet and assistants to respond more quickly when you arrive. Drive carefully!

Normal Vital Signs

- A dog's normal body temperature is 99.5°F-102.8°F.
- A dog's normal heart rate is 60-120 beats per minute.
- A dog normal respiration rate is 14-22 breaths per minute.

The veterinarian will cool your dog further if necessary, and administer fluids to help stabilize his temperature and prevent dehydration. She will also monitor your dog for body temperature, shock, respiratory problems, kidney damage, and other potential complications. Dogs usually recover completely from moderate heatstroke. Severe heatstroke can cause organ damage or death. A dog that has had heatstroke once is at higher risk of getting it again.

Summer Care Tips

Spring and summer bring a few other hazards besides heat. Here are some tips for keeping your Labrador Retriever safe and healthy in warm weather.

1. Risk of exposure to infectious diseases, including rabies, distemper, parvovirus, Lyme disease, and others, increases when the days warm up. Be sure your dog is protected.

2. Mosquitoes are active. If you live or travel in a part of the country that has heartworm, have your dog tested annually and give him heartworm preventative.

Insects, especially fleas and ticks, are very active in warm weather.

3. Insects, spiders, and other pests bite and sting dogs. If your dog has an allergic reaction to a bite or sting, or is bitten or stung several times, see a veterinarian as soon as possible.

4. Fleas and ticks are active in warm weather. Check your dog frequently for signs of fleas and ticks, and talk to your vet about appropriate treatment and prevention.

5. Insecticides, weed killers, mouse and rat poisons, fertilizers, and poisonous plants are all dangerous. Even if you don't use them in your home and yard, some of your neighbors probably do. If you think your dog has walked through grass treated with chemicals, wash his feet thoroughly with soap and warm water. If you think he's ingested a poison, get him to a vet.

6. Take care of your dog's feet–they burn as easily as yours do. Don't keep your dog on hot concrete, asphalt, or sand, or protect his feet with booties.

7. Labs love to swim, but keep it safe. Even good swimmers drown.

Keeping Your Lab Safe in Cold Weather

Colder weather also holds dangers for dogs, even Labs, who usually love to romp in the snow and will plunge into icy water just for the fun of it. Here are a few cold-weather tips to keep your Lab safe and healthy in winter.

1. Dogs, like people, are susceptible to frostbite, which occurs when a body part freezes. On a Lab, the most vulnerable areas are the ears, nose leather, and feet. If frostbite is not treated promptly, the affected areas die and may slough off or have to be amputated. Frostbitten skin is pale and cool to the touch. After it thaws, it may look like a burn. If you think your Lab has frostbite, warm the affected areas *slowly* and get him to a veterinarian as quickly as possible.

2. Jagged ice, frozen plant stems, and salt and other chemicals to promote melting are common hazards to your dog's feet in winter. Sharp edges can cut your dog's footpads, and salt and other chemicals can cause pads to dry and split. They'll also make your dog ill if he licks them off his feet. Check your dog's footpads frequently, and if he walks where salt or chemicals are used, wash his feet when he comes in.

Cold weather can be as dangerous as warm weather for your Lab.

3. If your Lab has a lot of hair between the pads of his feet, snow can collect on the hair and may form painful ice balls. If that is happening, trim the long hair from the bottoms of his feet so that it is level with his pads. Always check his feet when he comes in from the snow.

4. Icy surfaces, especially stairs and steps, are as dangerous for your dog as they are for you. Dogs with orthopedic problems or arthritis are especially at risk for falling on slippery surfaces. If your Lab is elderly or is not steady on his feet, try to provide an ice-free path from your door to his potty area.

5. Lakes, pools, ponds, and other bodies of water are extremely attractive to most Labs, even in icy weather, but they're also dangerous. Swimming in very cold water

A fenced-in dog run will keep your Lab from wandering off.

Your Lab needs lots of attention and playtime.

on cold days can cause *hypothermia,* or dangerous chilling of the body. Don't allow your Lab to swim in very cold water unless he's extremely fit and is a strong, experienced swimmer. Even then, monitor his condition carefully.

6. Bodies of water present another hazard as they freeze–thin ice is deceptive, and deadly. *Do not* allow your dog (or anyone else) to run on the icy surface of frozen water unless you know *for certain* that the ice is solid all the way across. If your dog falls through, he may not be able to find the hole again, or if he does, he may not be able to climb out. He could easily be caught under the ice and drown.

7. Be very careful if you walk your dog near snowmobile trails in winter. Keep him on leash and away from the trails. Snowmobiles can kill dogs–and you.

Confining Your Lab

Your Lab needs a properly fenced, secure area. If he's alone outside he may be tempted to chase a bird or squirrel or to wander off in search of company, and a fence will protect him from the dangers of running loose (which is also illegal in most parts of the country). A securely fenced and locked area will also protect your dog from other animals and may discourage would-be thieves or abusers. Outdoor dogs are frequently victims of theft, abuse, poisoning, teasing, and attack by other animals. A four-foot fence will hold most Labs, although some are jumpers or climbers and may need a higher barrier to keep them safely confined.

Don't tie or chain you Lab. Dogs who live tied up often develop a myriad of behavioral problems and are at the mercy of anyone and anything that passes by. If that's the only place you can keep a dog, please don't get one. *No dog deserves to live his life on a chain.*

Identifying Your Dog

Losing your dog is a terrible experience. Of course, you do everything possible to prevent that from happening. If it does, you want to be sure that your dog can be identified and you can be notified. A nametag with your telephone number attached to your dog's collar can be effective, but tags and collars can also be lost or removed. Tattoos or microchips provide permanent identification that can't be lost or easily remove, and a number of registry services provide 24-hour reporting and access. For more information, ask you veterinarian or contact:

Microchips

- PETtrac/AVID Microchips, (800) 336-AVID, 3179 Hamner Ave., Suite 5, Norco, CA 9176-9972
- HomeAgain Companion Animal Recovery, (800) 566-3596, Schering-Plough Animal Health, Attn: HomeAgain, 1095 Morris Avenue, P.O. Box 3182, Union, NJ 07083-1982, or (800) 252-7894, 5580 Centerview Drive, Suite 250, Raleigh, NC 27606-3394
- InfoPET, (800) INFOPET, 415 W. Travelers Trail, Burnsville, MS 55337

Tattoos

- Identipet, (800) 243-9147
- Tatoo-A-Pet, (800) 828-8667, 1625 Emmons Avenue, Brooklyn, NY 11235
- National Dog Registry, (800) NDR-DOGS

Tag Registration

- 1-800-Help-4-Pets, (800) HELP-PETS

Socialization

Socialization is essential to a puppy's development. Even though Labrador Retrievers are naturally very friendly, they will do better if you take the time to introduce them to many things while they are young. Don't forget that until he is fully vaccinated, your pup is vulnerable to common canine diseases. Even so, if you take reasonable precautions you can still get your puppy out to begin his education. Avoid high-risk environments, such as areas where stray or unvaccinated dogs may leave disease-carrying feces. Even if you have to carry him in some places, your pup may still meet people and see and hear lots of things.

Once he has finished his series of puppy shots, you can begin exposing your pup to all sorts of new things. Take him to lots of different places–parks, different neighborhoods, obedience classes, shopping centers, the sidewalk outside local stores–anywhere that he will see lots of people and things. Always keep him on leash in public places, of course, for his own safety and so that he doesn't bother people and other dogs that don't want to be

Did You Know?

Most people think that dogs and cats are natural enemies, but that's not necessarily true. Many cats and dogs live happily under the same roof and become quite friendly once they have been socialized properly.

bothered. Use these opportunities to reinforce his training–for instance, if he has learned to do a nice down-stay in less distracting circumstances like home and obedience class, start teaching him to do down-stays outside stores where people are passing.

If possible, enroll your pup in a puppy kindergarten class to give him a chance to interact with other puppies as well as people. Look for a class that offers positive reinforcement, and never punish a puppy. He's a baby, and he'll make mistakes. Think of mistakes as training opportunities. After all, he needs to learn what you *don't* want to fully understand what you *do* want. Guide him to the behavior you want, and reward him when he gets it right. The effort you make to socialize and begin training your Lab puppy while he's young will pay off later when he's a well-adjusted, mannerly companion.

Your Lab and Other Animals

Labrador Retrievers typically get along with just about anyone with two legs or four. But Labs, especially when they're puppies, can play rough and, big strong dogs that they are, they can easily overpower a lot of people and animals. It's important to teach your Lab to be polite, and to monitor his interactions, especially when he's young and rowdy.

If you already own a dog, introduce your new puppy to him gradually and supervise their interaction.

Your Lab Puppy and Your Current Dog

If you already have a dog (or dogs) in your home, you'll need to introduce your new puppy carefully. Keep control of all initial introductions, and supervise all interaction between your puppy and other dogs for at least the first few days. Puppies are serious little pests. Fortunately, well-socialized, kind-hearted adult dogs tolerate a lot of abuse from puppies. Puppies need to interact with adult dogs to learn how to be dogs. But it's not fair to expect your older pets to put up with too much from those sharp puppy teeth and claws. If an older dog gets fed up, he could frighten or injure the puppy. Puppies younger than four months old don't yet understand canine body language or manners, and they might not understand when another dog tells them to stop behaving like a puppy.

Be very careful about letting any adult dog that shows signs of aggressiveness interact with your puppy. If you have a dog that you already know is aggressive toward other dogs, be sure before you bring a puppy home that you'll be able to protect it. A puppy can be badly frightened and injured or even killed in an instant by an adult dog. Never leave a puppy alone with an adult dog unless you trust the adult completely, and even then, don't let the adult dog spend all his time with the pup–and don't forget that he needs private time with you too! Each dog should have his own food bowls and toys. Don't allow the puppy to bother the older dog when he's eating.

Introducing an Adult Lab

If your new Lab is an adult, he'll need some time to adjust to his new home. Many factors influence the adjustment time: the dog's basic personality, his past experiences, and the characteristics of your household will all be important. I've had adult rescued Labs walk into my house and act like they're home, whereas others may take a few days, or weeks, or even months to adjust completely. Patience, understanding, training, and love from you will make all the difference.

If You are bringing home an adult Lab, get him a crate so he has a place to call his own.

A Lab that has spent time in a shelter or running loose may take a little longer to adjust because of the stress he's experienced. Imagine being abandoned by the people you love and trust, or being lost, and then being locked up in a noisy place–how frightening! Some dogs have been through several changes in a short period of time–going from a home to a shelter to a new home. But Labs are wonderfully resilient and forgiving. Guide him patiently, and he'll soon consider you his best friend.

Spend lots of time with your new dog to accelerate the bonding process. If you already have a dog and the two get along, then go for walks, play, and hang out together. This will help your new dog merge into the pack. Be sure also to spend some time with each dog alone–each one deserves some private time to strengthen his individual bond with you and to make him feel *he's* your favorite dog in the world.

If he isn't already crate trained, get your new Lab a crate and teach him it's a nice place. Use it as you would use a crate for a puppy until you know you can trust the dog. An adult in a new place may resort to chewing, pottying, and other juvenile behaviors from the stress and insecurity of being in a new environment. If possible, put the crate in your bedroom at night, or near where your other dog sleeps–your new dog will soon feel right at home.

Labs and Cats

If you have a cat, introduce your new Lab, puppy or adult, cautiously, and keep control of the dog. Don't force a meeting. Let your cat decide how quickly the relationship will develop. Don't let the dog chase or play rough with the cat. If the dog gets pushy and the cat bops him, don't punish the cat! For her own safety, she needs to tell the dog what the limits are. A Lab, even as a puppy, is a big animal and can easily injure a cat even in play. Begin right away to teach your Lab to be gentle with the cat.

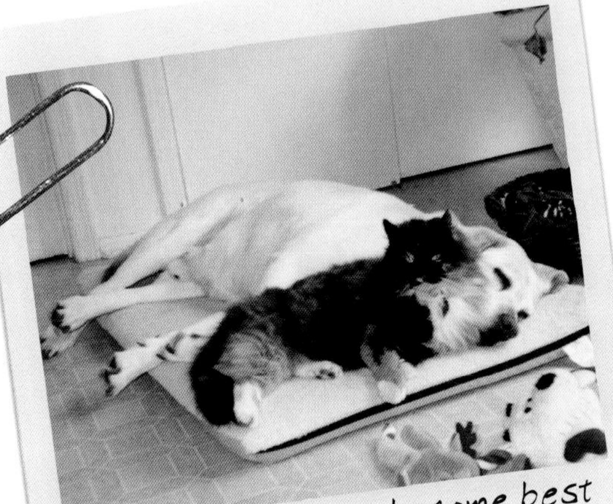

Dogs and cats can become best friends if they are raised together.

The dog-cat relationship will run more smoothly if you create "dog-free" zones where your cat can sleep, eat, play, and use the litter box without help from a nosy Lab. If your cat has a history of good experiences with dogs, things should be fine as soon as she sets down the rules. If your cat is not used to dogs, she may not be pleased about the newcomer for a while. When my husband, Roger, and I got married and I moved in with Raja, my Labrador Retriever, Roger's cat, Kitty, spent days on top of the refrigerator. A few weeks later, they were sleeping together on a big red dog bed. And yes, the names were confusing at first, but I had Raja first!

Socialization With Other Animals

In order to develop proper canine manners, your puppy needs to meet and interact with other dogs. The dilemma for owners of young puppies is how to start socializing the pup and still keep him safe from disease before his series of puppy shots is complete.

If you have an adult dog or two who are tolerant of the pup, then the socialization process has already begun at home. Let them interact, but supervise them for the first few weeks. Even the most patient of canine aunties and uncles can grow impatient when they're being assaulted with those puppy needle teeth. If you have friends with healthy, good-natured dogs that you know are good with puppies, invite them over (one at a time) for little play times. Be careful and supervise closely, of course. If the older dog seems less than delighted with your bouncing bundle of Labrador, don't force the issue.

Although he may one day be hunting these ducklings, this Lab loves being one of the flock.

Once your puppy has completed his puppy vaccination series, he can visit more places and meet more people and dogs. Be sensible, of course–don't let your puppy run wildly up to a dog he doesn't know. Most adult dogs will manage a silly puppy without hurting it, but it only takes one swift encounter with the wrong dog for your pup to be seriously injured or badly frightened. Besides, it's not fair to other dogs or people to let your dog just

A Word About Littermates

People sometimes think they'd like to get littermates and raise them together for companionship. Most breeders, however, discourage that practice. In general, puppies that are raised together, especially littermates, will bond tightly to one another and be less bonded to people. Raising two together may also complicate housetraining and other training.

If you really must raise littermates or same-age puppies together, the best approach for the first 18 months or so is to let them have an hour playtime together 2 or 3 times a day, but then separate them. Each one needs to learn to be alone with his toys at times. Each one also needs individual play and training time with his person or people.

If you want multiple dogs of about the same age, a better approach than raising littermates or age-mates is to get your first puppy, give him a good start, and when he's about 9 to 18 months old, bring home a second puppy.

Train you dog and your child to respect each other and play gently.

run up to them, no matter his age or size. You may know he's "just being friendly," but many people are afraid of dogs, and many dogs are not so friendly or tolerant.

Big Lab Puppies and Small Children

Labrador Retrievers are terrific family dogs, and many people buy Lab puppies as companions for their children. But happy puppy and child relationships don't just happen by themselves. Rough young puppies with sharp teeth and nails aren't born knowing how to behave with their new human companions. Nor are children born knowing that ears aren't for pulling and eyes aren't for poking. It's up to us to teach our puppies and our children.

All interaction between dogs and young children should be supervised closely by a responsible adult. That means the someone responsible is close enough to intervene immediately if necessary. Teach your puppy to sit or lie down for petting, and teach your children how to interact quietly with the pup without getting him all excited.

Spay or Neuter Your Child's Canine Companion

Altering—spaying females and neutering males—reduces the risk of biting in dogs of both sexes.

If you bring home a Lab puppy, he's bound to play rough, and he's armed with needle-sharp teeth and claws. Puppies aren't born knowing how to "play nice" with people. When they play with their littermates, puppies use their mouths and feet. They bite and pull and pounce. They enjoy making each other holler. Your puppy needs to learn that the rules are different when he plays with people, and that his teeth do not belong on human skin.

Children also need to be taught how to "play nice" with puppies and dogs. It's up to you to teach your kids that those velvety Labrador ears aren't for pulling and those big brown eyes aren't for poking. If you have an adult Lab–or adopt one–the same rules apply. Too many people assume that nice dogs will put up with anything a kid dishes out. And it's true–most Labs do put up with an awful lot without complaining. But it's not fair to your dog to allow children to hurt him, even if they don't mean to.

A responsible adult should supervise *all* interaction between a puppy and young children. The adult needs to be in a position to intervene immediately if necessary. Watching out the window from time to time is not enough. Things can get out of control much too quickly. Teach your puppy to sit or lie down to be petted. Teach him not to jump up on children and not to nip at ankles, hands, fannies, and faces. Teach your children how to interact with the pup without getting him all excited–no screaming or jumping around or running away, all of which will simply excite the pup more.

Older dogs and older children don't usually need such close supervision, but your older Lab should have obedience training, and your older children should understand that your dog is a living, feeling creature. Even a Labrador Retriever, tolerant as he is, can be provoked if he's teased or abused enough. Even if you don't have children of your own, teach your neighbor kids and don't allow them to tease or abuse you dog.

Part Two
Raising Your Labrador Retriever

"I sent him to fetch the paper last week, but he won't be putting it down until next Friday."

4

Living With a Labrador Retriever

Dogs are definitely high-maintenance companions. Your Lab depends on you for everything he needs, including proper nutrition, grooming, and exercise–all key elements in your Lab's health and well-being. Let's take a look at feeding, grooming, and exercising the Labrador Retriever throughout his life.

Choose the right food for your growing Lab puppy.

Nutrition & Feeding

The American market is overflowing with doggy diets ranging from very cheap foods that are nutritionally questionable, to high-priced "premium" foods, to homemade and raw-foods diets. Everywhere we look there are advertisements for dog foods. No matter what you choose to feed your dog, someone will tell

Your breeder should recommend a good food for your pup.

you it's bad for him. The best approach to feeding your dog well is to learn the basics of canine nutrition, as well as how to evaluate how your own dog seems to be doing on the food he eats.

Most breeders recommend feeding a high-quality dry dog food. Lab puppies should be fed either a puppy food specifically designed for large-breed dogs (more on puppy foods later), or adult or maintenance food. Excess protein and calcium in the diet can contribute to skeletal and joint problems, especially in puppies. Over-supplementation with vitamins, minerals, and other additives is a much more serious problem for most American dogs than is malnutrition. Never add nutritional supplements to your puppy's or dog's diet without first consulting your veterinarian.

Composition and Role of Food

The main ingredients of food are protein, fats, and carbohydrates. Food also contains vitamins and minerals, and, of course, water. Although all foods contain some of the basic ingredients needed for an animal to survive, they do not all contain those ingredients in the amounts or types needed by a specific type of animal. For example, many forms of protein are found in meats and plant matter. However, most plants contain "incomplete proteins" which lack certain amino acids that dogs require. Likewise, vitamins are found in meats and vegetation, but vegetables are a richer source of most vitamins than are meats. Vegetables are rich in carbohydrates, while meat is not.

Dogs are carnivores. The carnivore's digestive tract is designed to utilize meat proteins efficiently, and it cannot break down the tough cellulose walls of plant matter. In the wild, the carnivore eats nearly all of its prey, including the stomach containing partially digested food. Commercially prepared dog foods contain vegetables in which the cellulose has been broken down by cooking. Because vitamins are destroyed by the cooking, more vitamins are added back in after the heat process has been completed. It's important to feed a high-quality dog food to ensure complete nutrition for your dog–some of the cheaper brands don't offer complete nutrition, and your dog will pay the price with his health.

The food you feed your Lab should contain all the essential minerals, vitamins, fats, and proteins.

Proteins are made from amino acids, of which at least ten are essential if a puppy is to maintain healthy growth. Proteins provide the building blocks for the puppy's body. The richest sources are meat, fish, and poultry, together with their by-products, including milk, cheese, yogurt, fish meal, and eggs. Vegetable matter that has a high protein content includes soy beans, together with numerous corn and other plant extracts that have been dehydrated. Both the activity level of the dog and his age determine the actual protein content needed in the individual's diet. The total protein a dog needs to consume is also affected by how easily the food is digested.

Fats serve a number of purposes. They insulate internal organs against the cold and help protect the organs from knocks and bruises caused by normal activity. They provide a richer source of energy than any other food, and they transport vitamins and other nutrients to all the other organs via the blood. Finally, fat makes food palatable. Meats, meat by-products (milk and butter), and vegetable oils, such as safflower, olive, corn, or soybean, are all rich sources of fats.

Although fat is essential in the diet, it should not be excessive because the high energy content of fats (more than twice that of protein or carbohydrate) will increase the overall energy content of the diet. The dog normally adjusts its food intake to its energy needs, which are more easily met in a high-fat, high-energy diet. This means that a diet too high in fat will provide the dog's energy needs, but may not provide his protein, vitamin, and mineral needs.

Vitamins are chemical compounds that contribute to all aspects of an animal's health. Fruits are rich in vitamins, as are the livers of most animals. Many vitamins are unstable and easily destroyed by light, heat, moisture, or rancidity. Some vitamins, especially A and D, can be toxic in excessive doses. If you feed your Lab a high-quality food, his vitamins needs should be met. Don't add extra vitamins to your dog's diet unless your veterinarian advises you to do so. Hypervitaminosis (excess intake of vitamins) from supplements can cause serious, irreversible damage, especially in growing puppies.

Minerals (such as calcium, phosphorous, copper, iron, magnesium, selenium, potassium, zinc, and sodium) strengthen bones, teeth, and cell tissue and assist in metabolic processes. Unfortunately, canine mineral requirements have not been completely determined. As with vitamins, if you feed a good-quality diet, your Lab is unlikely to suffer a mineral deficiency. Excess minerals, on the contrary, can cause serious problems. Never add calcium or other minerals to a growing puppy's diet unless advised to do so by your veterinarian.

Water is essential to life and good health. Your adult dog is made up of about 60 percent water (even when he hasn't been swimming!), and puppies probably more. Your dog's daily total intake of water must be balanced by his total daily output of water. The intake comes directly from drinking, and indirectly as metabolic water, the water released from the food he eats. A healthy dog releases water primarily in his urine and his breath. If he's ill, he will lose water in vomiting and diarrhea as well. Your dog, like most animals, will lose condition more quickly from lack of water than from lack of food. You may want to restrict late-night water intake while housetraining a puppy, but otherwise your dog should have free access to clean water.

Your dog's activity level and age determine the amount of food he needs.

How Much Should I Feed?

The best way to tell whether your Lab is getting the right amount of food is by observing his general health and physical appearance. If he is well covered with flesh without being fat, shows good muscle and bone development, and is active and alert as expected for his age, he's probably eating the right amount of food. Because he's growing, a puppy needs about twice as much food as an adult of the same breed and size. If you're getting a puppy, ask the breeder how much he's been fed and use that as a starting point. Same with an adult–and adjust the portions as needed to keep him at a proper weight.

If your Lab starts to look fat–an all-too-common condition in Labs–then he is obviously overeating; the reverse is true if he starts to look excessively thin. Young puppies are roly poly, but by four months they should take on a fairly thin and lanky appearance which will last through adolescence. Don't let your Lab puppy be fat! Excess weight will exacerbate any genetic tendencies he may have to orthopedic problems. To determine if your dog's weight is appropriate, run your fingers down the sides of his spine. You should be able to feel the ribs. If you're in doubt, ask your vet.

A healthy dog should eat his meal in about five minutes. Use the manufacturer's recommendations for the amount to feed as a guideline only–and keep in mind that the amount recommended on the bag is often considerably more than most dogs need, especially if the dog gets treats in addition to its regular meals.

What About Puppy Foods?

Most "puppy" foods are packed with extra protein and calcium, not because puppies need them, but because puppy owners too often think more is better when reading dog food labels. Puppies, especially large-breed puppies like Labs, do not need the extra nutrients. In fact, they may suffer serious harm if fed too rich a diet. Extra protein and calcium cause faster bone growth. The problem is that the supportive soft tissues–tendons, ligaments, and muscles–cannot grow as fast as bones can. This disproportionate growth can permanently deform the bones and rupture the connections among the tissues and bone.

Veterinarians and breeders of large-breed puppies usually recommend that you *do not* follow manufacturers' recommendations to feed puppy food throughout the first year. Instead, most suggest that you either start right out with a good-quality adult or all-age formula, or feed puppy food until the pup is about four months old and then switch to adult food.

Nutritional Supplements

Oversupplementation with vitamins, minerals, and other additives can cause serious health problems. In nutrition, more is usually not better! *Never* add nutritional supplements to your puppy's or dog's diet without first consulting your veterinarian.

Feeding Schedules

Some people "free feed" their puppies and dogs, which means the bowl is kept full and the pup has free access to food most or all of the time. There are several problems with free feeding. First, it frequently leads to obesity, especially in Labs, who are notorious eaters and weight-gainers. Second, free feeding

Setting up a regular feeding schedule will help with housetraining.

interferes with effective housetraining because the puppy that has no regular eating schedule also has no regular elimination schedule. Third, if you are using motivational training methods that involve treats, a constantly full dog may not be as interested as one that is a bit hungry before meal times. Finally, the first sign of illness is often lack of appetite, and that may be hard to spot if your pup isn't expected to eat promptly when fed.

Scheduled feeding involves feeding the dog at more or less the same time every day. In older, housetrained dogs, the schedule doesn't need to be rigid. In puppies that are being housetrained, however, a regular eating schedule makes for a regular elimination schedule, and that makes housetraining much easier. Scheduled feedings also allow you to control your puppy's food intake and weight much more easily, and training shortly before meals makes for a highly motivated pup. Finally, if your pup becomes ill and stops eating, you will know very quickly, perhaps before other symptoms appear.

Food and the Labrador Retriever Puppy

Good early nutrition is essential for proper development of a puppy's mind and body. For the first three to four weeks, puppies are nursed by their dams (unless unusual circumstances require the breeder to step in and hand-feed them). Even if you never have newborn puppies to care for, it's worthwhile to understand a bit about a puppy's early nutritional needs. After all, your puppy's life didn't start the day you brought him home. It started the day he was conceived. The care his breeder provided for his dam and her puppies throughout her pregnancy and the first weeks of his life will have a lifelong effect on your dog's physical and mental health. This is another reason to shy away from carelessly bred Labs. Prenatal care is important for doggies, too!

Weaning

Most breeders begin feeding their puppies when they are about four weeks old. Some force-wean their puppies at four to six weeks by removing the dam for several days until her milk dries up. Her own food intake is cut back drastically during this time in order to discourage milk production, while the puppies learn to rely exclusively on food provided by the breeder. Other breeders prefer to give the dam free access to the pups throughout the first seven to ten weeks. In the latter case, as the puppies gain more and more of their nourishment from food provided by the breeder, the bitch will need less food and will produce less milk. She will also likely grow tired of her nursing pups' sharp little teeth and she will begin to discourage them from nursing. Weaning will take place gradually and naturally.

Many breeders begin to wean their puppies at four to six weeks of age.

First Diet

First diets for puppies vary from elaborate blends mixed up by breeders to puppy food soaked in water. At first, the food needs to be fairly soupy, but as their teeth become more evident, you can cut back on the water content of their food. By six or seven weeks, they should be able to eat dry puppy food with no problem as long as they have access to plenty of clean water. If you are feeding a young litter, speak to the breeder from whom you bought your bitch, or other experienced breeders, for feeding advice, and consult your veterinarian. As long as the puppies are getting an adequate amount of good quality food, whether homemade or commercial, they'll do fine.

Feeding the Growing Puppy

Young puppies are normally fed three or four times a day, and should be offered as much food as they will eat in a reasonable amount of time. The dam should be removed from the puppy feeding area while they are eating to prevent her scarfing up all their food, but she may be allowed in to clean the bowls afterwards–and to clean her pups! At first, many puppies show no interest in drinking water, but clean water should always be available to them once they start to eat. Sooner or later they'll start drinking it. Being Labs, they'll probably wade in it, too!

Did You Know?

If you feed your Lab the recommended serving size at each meal as well as give him handfuls of treats each day, you are overfeeding him. Treats should be counted as part of his daily food intake—not in addition to it.

Food and the Adult Labrador Retriever

Good nutrition is vital to your Lab's health not just while he's growing but throughout his life. A high-quality diet fed in the proper amount will go a long way toward keeping your dog healthy and active well into his senior years.

An adolescent or adult Labrador doesn't need to be fed as many times a day as a puppy.

Feeding the Adolescent Lab

Older puppies and adult dogs should be fed twice daily. Feeding times should be fairly regular, although once the pup is housetrained, you don't need to be quite so rigid. The specific times don't matter, and can be fit into your regular schedule. Keeping regular feeding times and feeding set amounts will help you monitor your puppy's or dog's health and control his weight. If a dog that's normally enthusiastic about mealtimes suddenly shows a lack of interest in food, you'll know immediately that something is wrong.

Preventing Weight Gain

Labrador Retrievers are notoriously prone to obesity, especially as they age. Don't let your Lab get fat! Obesity will shorten his life, and make the time he has less comfortable. If your dog has arthritis, as many older Labs do, extra weight will make him ache that much more.

To keep your older guy fit and trim, you need to provide him with proper nutrition and proper exercise. As long as he doesn't suffer a medical condition that prevents him from exercising, try to keep him active with daily walks, swimming if possible, and maybe a gentle game of fetch the ball. Activity will keep his muscles toned, which will in turn support his skeletal system and burn calories more efficiently.

If you see that he's gaining weight, cut back a little on the amount of food you are feeding him. If he still seems to be hungry, add some unsalted green beans, canned pumpkin (just the vegetable, not pie filling!), or air-popped unsalted popcorn to fill him up. You might also try giving him three or four smaller meals through the day rather than one or two bigger ones–just be sure that the total amount of food doesn't increase. Speak to your vet about a weight-loss or lower calorie food if you are unable to take or keep the weight off your Lab.

Grooming for Good Health

Even though Labs are relatively low-maintenance in the grooming department, they do need some care. Grooming includes bathing, coat care, eye/ear care, nail care, and dental care. Grooming can be a special time for you and your Lab. While he's a puppy, grooming will teach him to trust you and enjoy your touch. When he's grown, he'll continue to love your hands on him and the time you spend together.

Most Labs don't need to be bathed very often, but from time to time you'll want to bathe your dog. Use a good quality shampoo made for dogs. Don't use human shampoos–the pH is wrong for dogs' skins. Use lukewarm water. Cold water can chill him, and most Labs dislike water that's too warm. Be sure to rinse your dog thoroughly as soap residue can cause serious skin irritations. Keep your puppy or elderly dog warm and out of drafts until he dries. If you use any grooming or flea-prevention products on your puppy, be sure to read all instructions and warning labels. Not all products are suitable or safe for puppies or for dogs with health problems.

Most Labs enjoy being groomed, especially if you are gentle and you make this an enjoyable time to spend together, not an ordeal to survive. During the spring and fall, your Lab will shed more than at other times, and an undercoat rake will help pull out a lot of the hair quickly. Otherwise, a slicker brush (a flat brush with metal pins) does a nice job on the body–just don't press too hard or you'll be scraping skin rather than brushing fur.

Even though Labs are relatively low-maintenance dogs, they still need some care.

It's also important to teach your puppy early to accept nail clipping. Allowing the nails to grow too long can cause serious, permanent damage to the foot, so nails should be trimmed every three to four weeks, depending on the individual dog. If you're teaching your puppy or new adult dog to accept nail trimming, you need to do a little trimming more frequently to get him used to it. Handle his feet frequently when you're not doing his nails so that he doesn't assume the worst when you touch his feet. Start by trimming one or two nails per session, and then rewarding him with a belly rub and maybe a small treat. Do two more nails the next day. He'll quickly learn to accept nail trimming as no big deal.

If you are unsure of how to trim the nails, have your veterinarian, breeder, or a groomer show you the proper angle and length. As a last resort, if you are truly uncomfortable clipping your dog's nails, you can have them done at the vet's office or by a groomer.

If you plan to show your Lab, speak to your dog's breeder about proper care and grooming for the show ring. The Labrador Retriever is judged in part on a proper double coat, with dense undercoat for insulation and hard, oily outer coat for water repellence. Improper or too-frequent bathing can damage the texture of the show coat.

Dental Care

More than 80 percent of dogs over 3 years of age have symptoms of gum disease. Gum disease contributes to bad breath, tooth loss, and other serious problems. Bacteria can enter the bloodstream through diseased gums and damage your dog's heart, kidneys, and other organs. So regular preventive dental care is vital to your Labrador Retriever's overall health.

Examine your dog's teeth for tartar and plaque buildup.

Your veterinarian can show you how to brush your dog's teeth properly, recommend safe dental care products, and help you design a good home dental care regimen. Toothpaste intended for people can cause stomach upsets when swallowed, so use a product made for dogs. You can also buy a specially designed doggy toothbrush, or clean your dog's teeth with a piece of surgical gauze wrapped around your fingers and dampened with water. You can add a little baking soda or doggy toothpaste to the gauze if you like.

Regular dental checkups should be part of your dog's

routine care. Your dog should have his teeth cleaned and polished by your vet as often as necessary. If your dog has symptoms of bad breath, visible tartar along the gum line, bleeding gums, or other problems in or around his mouth, have your vet take a look.

Ear Care

Labrador Retrievers are, unfortunately, prone to ear infections. Some ear infections are bacterial. Yeast infections are also very common, especially if your Lab swims or plays in water–which he will, given half a chance–or if you have another dog that likes to lick his ears. The warm, moist environment of the Lab's ear, covered as it is by the ear "leather" or flap, promotes the abnormal growth of yeast. Not all Labs get ear infections, but in some Labs they become chronic, especially if preventive care isn't practiced on a regular basis.

Homemade Ear Cleaning Solutions

Here are two inexpensive, easy-to-make ear cleaning solutions to keep your Lab's ears clear of infections. The rubbing alcohol helps to dry out the ear, and both solutions help to make the environment of the ear inhospitable to bacteria and yeast. Use one or the other.

Note: These solutions are not meant to clear up an existing infection. If your dog develops an ear infection, take him to your veterinarian.

Solution 1:

- 1 part rubbing alcohol
- 1 part white vinegar

Shake well. Use generously to flush the ear. Use once a month or more frequently if needed.

Solution 2:

- 2 tablespoons Boric Acid
- 4 oz Rubbing Alcohol
- 1 tablespoons Glycerine

Shake well. Apply with an eyedropper—one dropper-full in each ear. Massage, then let the dog shake well

If Your Lab develops an ear infection, see Your vet. Correct diagnosis is essential.

Check your Lab's ears regularly. The skin inside the ear should appear pink or flesh toned and clean and should not look inflamed. There should be no strong or nasty odor from the ear canal. If the ear appears inflamed or seems sensitive when you handle it, or if there is a foul smell, take your dog to the vet. It's essential to identify the type of infection in order to treat it effectively. Over-the-counter treatments for the wrong type of ear infection will simply prolong your dog's discomfort and may allow the infection to become so well established that proper treatment later will be more difficult.

If your Lab's ear is dirty, you can clean it with a commercial or homemade cleaner . Squirt plenty of cleaner into the ear to flush it out, then close the earflap over the ear and massage for a few second to work the cleaner well into the ear canal. Then stand back! The dog will shake his head, throwing the cleaner and dirt far and wide. Ear cleaning is best done outdoors or in a bathroom or other area where cleanup will be easy. After both ears are flushed and shaken, gently wipe them out with a tissue or cotton ball. *Do not* poke cotton swabs into your dog's ears. If your dog's ears seem to generate a lot of wax, or if he introduces water into his ears frequently from swimming, then clean them about once a week to forestall bacteria and yeast. If his ears are healthy, once a month cleaning will help keep them that way.

Daily exercise and play are important in maintaining optimum health.

Exercise

Labrador Retrievers are energetic dogs and need adequate exercise to be at their best physically, mentally, and emotionally. This is especially true through adolescence and young adulthood. On the other hand, your puppy's bones will still be growing until he is about a year old, at which time the growth plates close. Some cautions are in order when exercising young Labs.

Growth plates (also called epiphyseal plates or the epiphysis) are soft areas of immature bone found near the ends of the puppy's leg bones. Growth–mainly lengthening–of the bones comes from the growth plates. Around one year of age, calcium and minerals harden the soft area in a process usually referred to as the closing of the growth plates. Most growth comes to an end at this time.

The soft growth plates in young dogs are vulnerable to fractures and other injuries. As long as the growth plates are open, you need to monitor the type of exercise your Lab engages in and discourage high-impact and leg-twisting activities such as jumping, leaping after flying disks, and so forth. Fortunately there are lots of less hazardous activities for your rambunctious young Lab!

Labrador Retrievers love the water and usually learn to swim easily.

Swimming

Labrador Retrievers love water and usually learn to swim easily. Of course, puppies have to learn how to swim, and each pup needs to learn at his own rate so that he doesn't become frightened. Let your puppy wade and splash. Don't try to rush things–if he has a good time, he'll go in deeper next time. The best place to introduce a pup to water is at a dogs-allowed beach with a gentle slope into the water and little or no current. Remember, although adult Labs that are fit and used to swimming can handle fairly strong currents, puppies don't have the strength for difficult water. If you have an older dog that likes to swim, your Lab puppy will probably follow suit gleefully. Never throw a young puppy into the water! It's our responsibility to keep puppies safe and to provide them with positive experiences.

If you have a swimming pool, never allow your dog access to the pool without a responsible adult around. Dogs often cannot easily pull themselves out of the pool and even strong swimmers will tire if they can't find an easy way out of the water. Tired dogs sometimes drown. Similarly, if you have a pool cover, be absolutely certain that it's Lab-proof–dogs have been known to slip under pool covers from the side or to go through covers and drown. If you do let your Lab in your swimming pool when you're there to supervise, check that filter often. Labs shed much more than people do.

Living With Your Labrador Senior Citizen

Old dogs are very special. As I write this, I'm surrounded by dogs in their second decades, including my sweet yellow Lab, Annie. Aging gives a dog a special dignity, and your Lab

How Your Lab's Age Translates to Human Ages

Age in Years	Approximate Equivalent Age in Humans
5	40
6	45
7	50
8	55
9	61
10	66
11	72
12	77
13	82
14	88
15	93
16	99

deserves your love and attention in his later years as much as he did when he was younger–maybe more.

Feeding the Senior Lab

Most dog food manufacturers offer "light" and "senior" lines of foods, but there is no scientific evidence that the reduced protein content of most geriatric foods is beneficial for older dogs. If your senior Lab is staying at a proper weight and his skin and coat are healthy, there is probably no good reason to switch him to a different formula just because he is aging.

Dehydration, which can contribute to serious health problems, is often a problem for elderly dogs. If your Lab has arthritis or for some other reason has trouble getting around, he may not go to his water bowl often enough. Try to monitor his water intake to be sure he's drinking enough water. If he has trouble getting around, consider placing an extra water bowl or two in different locations so that it's easier for him to get a drink. If you notice that he hasn't been drinking, carry some water to him and offer him some. Be sure the water he has is clean–if you wouldn't drink it, don't expect him to. Your older Lab's kidneys aren't as tolerant of impurities as they used to be, so it's vital that he drink good, clean water.

Senior Labs need just as much attention as pups. Don't neglect your aging dog.

Many older dogs are less interested in food than they were when younger. If your aging Lab loses his appetite gradually, he's probably just losing interest in food because his senses of smell and taste are less acute. You can encourage him to eat if necessary by making his food more appealing. Serve it at room temperature or slightly warmer (don't serve it to him hot–you don't want him to burn his mouth). Warmer food is more fragrant than cold, therefore it's more inviting. A little water or unsalted broth, plain yogurt, or cottage cheese added to his food may also make it more interesting.

Be sure, too, that your dog can reach his food comfortably. If he has arthritis, lowering his head to his bowl at floor level may be painful. If that seems to be the case, elevate his food and water bowls to just below the height of his mouth when he's standing. Pet supply stores offer a variety of food stands or you can easily make one by cutting a circle the size of the bowl into the bottom of a plastic wastebasket and standing the basket upside down.

A problem in his mouth or throat may also make eating uncomfortable for your senior, so if he stops eating, check his teeth, gums, tongue, and the roof of his mouth. If your dog suddenly loses his appetite or is losing a lot of weight, check with your vet.

Exercise

As your Labrador Retriever ages, he will probably lose that adolescent rowdiness he once had, but he still needs to exercise to remain physically, mentally, and emotionally healthy. Obesity is a major problem in adult Labs and lack of sufficient exercise is a major contributor to life-shortening excess weight. Coupled with a proper diet, exercise

Your older Lab still needs exercise to remain in good health.

appropriate to your dog's general health and condition will help keep his weight down, his cardiovascular and digestive systems healthy, and his muscles toned. Exercise will also make your dog happier and alleviate boredom, and walks and games of fetch will keep the bond between you strong.

A ten-year-old Lab may not be able to run as fast and as far as he once could, and, like his human counterparts, he may not always admit that he's not as young as he used to be. As his friend and caretaker, you need to monitor his health and fitness. If your Lab is over seven and has not been exercising regularly, take him to your vet for a checkup and geriatric screening before beginning an exercise program.

Don't let your old dog get so carried away with the fun of the game, or because he wants to please you, that he hurts himself. Coughing or loss of breath during or after exercise can indicate a heart problem and should be reported to your veterinarian. If your Lab has orthopedic problems, such as hip or elbow dysplasia, or has arthritis, check with your vet about appropriate exercise. Swimming is good for a dog with joint problems if he's otherwise healthy, but can be risky for a dog with heart problems. An older dog is more susceptible to chilling than a younger one, so limit swimming to warm days and reasonably warm water. Your Lab may have loved a plunge into icy water in his younger years, but cold water isn't good for an old dog. Walking is also excellent exercise and easier on the joints than running.

Monitor your Lab's weight carefully as he ages. Dogs, like people, require less food to maintain their weight as they age, so adjust his food intake as needed to keep his weight down. Excess weight will shorten your Lab's life and make the time he has less comfortable.

Activities for the Senior Lab

If your senior Lab is still in reasonably good health and remains physically fit, there are activities in which he can still participate. Doing so will give you quality time together and will help keep him interested in life–a good thing for older Labs as well as people.

There's no reason for your dog to stop participating in obedience or other sports if he's still healthy and seems to enjoy the activity. Many older dogs also participate in dog-assisted therapy work, visiting nursing homes, hospitals, and schools.

As your Lab ages, he'll tolerate extreme temprature changes less easily than when he was younger.

Other Considerations for Your Older Labrador Retriever

As your Lab grows older, he'll tolerate extremes of temperature less easily than when he was younger. He may still think he's a tough guy, so it's up to you to protect him from risky exposure to cold, wet conditions that could chill him. In hot weather, he may have more trouble cooling himself than he used to, especially if he's picked up some excess weight, so be sure he has a cool place when it's hot out, and that he has access to clean, cool water all the time.

Give your older Lab a comfy bed to sleep on. "Egg-crate" or "orthopedic" mattresses offer comfortable support for arthritic dogs. You can purchase them from most pet supply stores and discount stores, or purchase the egg-crate foam made for people's beds and cut it to an appropriate size. Some dogs prefer a looser sort of bedding that they can dig and scrunch and then sink into, so watch your dog to see what sort of bed he likes. If there's room in your bed, you may find that's his favorite place for a snooze!

Saying Goodbye

Saying goodbye to loved ones is never easy, but eventually most dog owners must do so. As your Lab ages, the quality of his life may eventually decline due to any of the number of diseases and conditions that affect elderly dogs. When he reaches a point at which he is in severe pain or obviously has more bad days than good, you may want to discuss the possibility of euthanasia with your veterinarian. If your dog is terminally ill or badly injured and proper care is beyond your means, euthanasia is preferable to allowing him to suffer. The decision to have a beloved dog euthanized is difficult, emotional, and very personal. Only you and your family know what's right for your and your dog.

Ten Tips for Keeping Your Older Lab Healthy

1. Take your dog to the vet every 6 to 12 months, depending on your dog's health.
2. Discuss your dog's vaccination schedule with your vet, and try not to over- or under-vaccinate.
3. Tell your vet immediately if you see changes in your dog's behavior or condition.
4. Feed your dog the best food you can afford, and keep your dog at a healthy weight.
5. See that your dog gets regular exercise as appropriate for his age and condition.
6. See that your dog has regular dental care.
7. Keep your dog's living quarters clean.
8. Keep your dog free of internal and external parasites.
9. Groom your dog regularly, and keep his nails properly trimmed.
10. Spend quality time with your dog, and make sure he remains as much a part of your life as ever.

When you must say goodbye to your Lab friend, always remember the fun times you shared.

Euthanasia nearly always involves injecting a drug that will immediately put your dog into irreversible unconsciousness, followed very quickly by death. I believe that a painless, dignified passage is a gift we are able to give. If you can stay with your dog and whisper goodbye, it will be that much easier for him.

Unless your dog is suffering from accidental injury or a sudden, acute medical problem, you'll have time to decide. Talk to your vet and your family about your dog's condition, chances for recovery, medical options, and quality of remaining life with your vet and your family. Let all your family members voice their feelings, including children. They usually accept death better than we adults anticipate, but they need to be part of the family process. Let everyone say goodbye in his or her own way, privately if they wish, and recognize that grieving is necessary and normal.

Ceremonies are useful to bring a sense of closure for those who loved your dog, so consider doing something symbolic. Perhaps you can cremate your dog's remains and display them, or bronze his collar or favorite toy. You might make a donation to a Labrador Retriever rescue group, a local shelter, Labrador health research, or another charitable cause in honor of your Lab. Creating a scrapbook about your dog is therapeutic for many people, especially children.

5

Health Care and First Aid

Overall, the Labrador Retriever is a hardy breed, but like all living things, Labs are susceptible to inherited and acquired health problems. The wise buyer takes the time to become informed about problems and realizes that it pays both financially and emotionally to do business only with breeders who screen their breeding animals. Don't let the list of major problems seen in Labs frighten you–there *are* healthy Labrador Retrievers! Being an informed and responsible buyer will greatly increase your chances of finding a Lab that is healthy in mind and body.

Choose a vet carefully to make sure your dog gets the best care possible.

Your Vet: Partner for Your Lab's Life

The time to select a veterinarian is before your new Labrador joins your family. You should feel

Ask friends, family, and especially your breeder for recommendations on choosing a vet.

as confident and comfortable with your dog's vet as you do with your child's pediatrician or your own physician. Ideally, you and your dog will enjoy a long-term relationship with your veterinarian, which will help give continuity to your dog's care. Of course, if you find you are uncomfortable with your vet or with the atmosphere or policies of the practice, you may want to switch. If you move you may have to find a new vet. But overall it will be to your dog's advantage to see the same vet most of the time. Your vet will keep a medical history on your dog, including a record of immunizations, conditions and treatments, reactions, and so forth. As your dog grows older, a long-term view of his medical history may be important.

So how can you find your ideal veterinarian if you haven't already? If you are acquiring your Lab from a local breeder or rescue program, ask for recommendations. Ask friends

Ten Things to Keep in Mind When Choosing a Veterinary Hospital

1. Are the facilities clean and well organized?
2. Are the office hours compatible with your schedule?
3. What services (grooming, boarding, and so forth) does the hospital provide?
4. Are the receptionists competent and friendly in person and on the phone?
5. Can you request a specific veterinarian?
6. Do you feel comfortable the veterinarian?
7. Do the doctors and the hospital members belong to any professional veterinary associations?
8. Who will see your pet if your regular veterinarian isn't available?
9. How are emergencies handled during regular office hours and after hours?
10. Are you informed about and comfortable with the practice's policies?

who have dogs–particularly Labrador Retrievers–about their vets. When you sign your puppy or dog up for obedience or other classes, ask the instructors for recommendations. If you belong to a dog club, especially a Labrador Retriever breed club, ask other members for recommendations. Ask people what they like and don't like about their vets and about the practices in which their vets work, keeping in mind that your needs and ideas about your dog's care may be different from theirs. The personalities of vets, dogs, and clients also come into play–not all vets work well with large, rambunctious dogs. As a last resort, check the telephone book or Internet for local veterinarians.

Once you identify two or three veterinary practices or specific vets who seem to be possibilities, visit their facilities. Ask for a tour of the clinic or hospital, and ask to interview the vet you are considering. It's worth the price of an office call (usually around $25) to find out whether you feel comfortable with you dog's future health care provider. Take a list of questions along. If you are interested in alternative therapies, reduced vaccination schedules, or natural diets, discuss the vet's position on them. If being thoroughly informed about your dog's health is important to you, the veterinarian's reaction to your general interview questions will be an indicator of how she will react to specific questions and concerns in the future.

Remember, too, that we are responsible for helping our veterinarians diagnose and treat our animals. We need to observe the subtle behaviors and symptoms in our dogs and communicate that information accurately to our vets for the most effective health care.

Littermates love to sleep close to each other.

The Healthy Labrador Retriever Puppy

Newborn Health

The first week of a puppy's life is critical in terms of survival. Although a healthy newborn puppy is remarkably strong and vibrant, he is also extremely vulnerable to a host of life-threatening situations. Many puppies die during their first week or two from difficulties during the birth, congenital or genetic problems, infection, viruses, toxic milk, malnourishment, a too-cold or too-warm environment, or even carelessness of the dam. Careful management, though, can greatly increase the puppies' chances of surviving.

Newborn puppies can't regulate their own body temperature and are therefore at risk of becoming too warm or too cold. Hypothermia (chilling) is, in fact, one of the leading causes of death in newborns. If a puppy is cool to the touch, feel his tongue–a cool tongue means a chilled puppy. Warm him slowly by placing him under a moderate heat lamp or on a warm (never hot) heating pad designed for newborn animals (heating pads for people are too warm and can kill a puppy), or tuck him up against his mom or yourself for a while. *Never feed a chilled puppy*–his digestive system won't work until he warms up, and the milk in his stomach can kill him. Newborn puppies should be kept in an environment of 85°F to 90°F. Heating pads and heat lamps designed for use with newborn animals can be used, but always keep a thermometer in the whelping area and monitor the temperature closely. Too much heat can dehydrate puppies and kill them.

Puppies should be weighed at birth, and then weighed every day for the first week and once a week after that. It's quite normal for a pup to lose a little weight the first day, but from then on he should gain steadily and should double his weight in seven to ten days. Puppies should nurse vigorously starting very soon after birth. If a puppy is not breathing regularly and seems lethargic, rub him briskly with a towel, and if that doesn't do the trick, put a drop of brandy on his tongue. Failure to nurse, weight loss or insufficient weight gain, drop in body temperature, dehydration, continuous crying, diarrhea, and vomiting are all signs of serious trouble in neonates–call your vet if they occur.

No one should breed a litter casually. There are a number of excellent books and websites devoted to breeding. If you plan to breed, educate yourself and plan ahead for the normal course of events and for emergencies.

Some routine care is required for healthy newborns. The umbilical cord should be swabbed daily with iodine or rubbing alcohol to prevent infection and encourage drying. This is especially critical during the first 24 hours to prevent infection. The cord should dry up and fall off in two or three days. If it appears soft or discolored, call your veterinarian immediately–puppies die of umbilical infection without intervention.

Check the dam's milk supply regularly. If puppies are tugging on nipples and crying, the bitch may not be producing enough milk. Some bitches actually produce too much milk, and can develop mastitis, or infection of the breast, that can threaten mother and pups. Check your bitch's breasts daily–they should feel comfortably full and warm, but not feverishly hot or hard. If the breasts don't seem normal, take your bitch's temperature. Normal temperature is around 101.5°F. If her temperature is 103°F or higher, call your vet immediately. Infected breasts can abscess, causing pain and potentially more serious problems for the dam, and the milk can poison the pups.

A Healthy Newborn Puppy:

√ Looks and feels strong, vigorous and firm—"like a hand in a glove"

√ Nurses with great gusto

√ Breathes freely

√ Feels and looks full but not bloated

√ Feels warm to the touch and has a warm, pink tongue

√ Twitches in his sleep to prepare his muscles and nervous systems for further development (called "activated sleep")

Puppies cannot eliminate on their own for the first two weeks. Normally, the dam licks them to stimulate urination and defecation. If for some reason she is unable to do so, you must step in. Use a damp cotton ball and stroke the anus until the pup has a bowel movement and the genitals until the puppy piddles. This must be done every two to three hours and after each feeding.

Puppies eyes are sealed shut for the first 7 to 14 days. The lids should look clean. If the eyes look swollen or if there is discharge from the corners, check with your veterinarian. The eyes may require treatment to prevent permanent damage. The ears are similarly sealed until the pup is 7 to 14 days old. The ears, like the eyes, should look clean.

A Sick Newborn Puppy:

√ Looks and feels weak, lethargic, and limp

√ Stops nursing completely or partially

√ Breathes irregularly or noisily

√ Feels and looks bloated or empty

√ Feels cool to the touch and has a cool, pale tongue

√ Lies still when sleeping

√ Cries a lot

√ Has diarrhea

√ Vomits repeatedly

Early Development

Puppies are completely dependent on their dam or foster dam for their first two weeks. They cannot see, hear, or eliminate without stimulation. They react reflexively to hunger and touch. They cannot cool themselves by panting or warm themselves by shivering, so their breeder must see that the environment around them is neither too warm nor too cold. Involuntary twitching, called "activated sleep," as well as crawling and head swinging, help neonatal puppies gain strength and prepare for further neurological development. The puppies rely on their dam to clean them and feed them. And their dam depends on the breeder for proper nutrition, privacy, and clean quarters for her family. Good breeders also give their bitches plenty of emotional support and cuddles.

Studies show that gentle handling and very light stimulation, sometimes terms "early neurological stimulation," help neonatal puppies to develop more brain cells, which helps them learn better later on. If you're buying a puppy, ask the breeder what sort of early handling and stimulation she gave her puppies.

Puppies change a lot during their third week. Their eyes and ears open, and they start to respond to light, movement, and sounds. They should be protected from loud noises, sudden movements, and bright lights (including camera flashes) during this time. Puppies are very mobile, and they crawl all around their den. They start getting on their feet, swaying, staggering, and falling down as they learn to use those wobbly legs. Puppies at this age are very much aware of their dam and siblings, objects in their area, and people. They are growing fast, and by the end of the third week, some are trying to play with toys and one another. A few brave little souls may try to escape the whelping box to explore that great big inviting world. The third week is a good time for the breeder to introduce puppies to a soft brush and to start regular nail trimming. Prospective show pups can also be placed briefly on a grooming table while getting lots of petting.

Puppies are ready to leave for their new home around 7 weeks of age.

Puppies go through significant changes from the fourth through the seventh week. They learn how to form social bonds and how to communicate–in short, they learn how to be dogs. Play fighting–some of it not so playful–develops and intensifies. Puppies sort themselves into a dominance hierarchy within the litter, based on personality and strength. They also begin to recognize and respond to people in the fourth week. Their problem-solving skills are developing and can be encouraged with toys and small obstacles such as cardboard boxes, barriers to go around, steps, and so forth. They become more coordinated physically. They begin to learn that they can't do anything they want as the dam disciplines them for being too pushy or rough. Puppies learn to inhibit, or control, the urge to bite from their dam and siblings, who don't like being bitten.

Pups are usually introduced to food during the fourth week, and they begin to move away from their eating and sleeping areas to urinate and defecate. The breeders can encourage

First Aid Kit for Dogs

Emergencies can happen in the blink of an eye—usually on Saturday just after your veterinarian's office has closed for the weekend. Having basic first aid supplies and some critical phone numbers easily at hand can make all the difference.

Here are the basics of a good doggy first aid kit:

√ A muzzle to keep your dog from biting when excited or in pain

√ A fresh bottle of hydrogen peroxide 3% (USP)

√ Turkey baster, bulb syringe or large medicine syringe for administering appropriate purgative

√ Saline eye solution to flush out eye contaminants

√ Artificial tear gel to lubricate eyes after flushing

√ Pepto Bismal

√ Topical antibiotic

√ Mild grease-cutting dishwashing liquid in order to bathe an animal after skin contamination

√ Rubber gloves to prevent you from being exposed while you bathe the animal

√ Forceps to remove stingers

√ A crate in which to transport your dog safely to a veterinarian

√ Good basic veterinary first aid manual

√ Small notebook and pen or pencil for noting anything that might be of significance (for instance, time poison was ingested, time of a seizure, etc.)

√ Telephone numbers of your veterinarian, closest emergency veterinary facility, and the National Animal Poison Control Center (NAPCC)—1-888-4ANI-HELP or 1-900-680-000 this "cleanliness urge" and help with future housetraining by keeping the puppies in clean surroundings and by taking them outdoors to eliminate from the fourth or fifth week on, depending on the weather.

Sensory development speeds up during the fourth week. Puppies are alert and easily startled at this age, so it's important to protect them from loud noises and other things that might frighten them and have long-lasting effects. This is a critical time developmentally, as puppies learn quickly and remember most of what they learn. Breeders who provide an enriched environment with varying toys, rolled-up towels to crawl over, shredded newspaper to dig through, steps to climb, and other play things give their puppies a head start on later learning. Exposing puppies to new sounds on the radio and television and other noisy things helps their social and mental development.

During the fifth through seventh weeks, puppies learn many things they will need to know to become well-adjusted adults. Each pup should get some individual attention away from the litter at this time, but most of the puppies' time should be spent together. Puppies should not leave the litter any earlier than the end of the seventh week, and the dam should have access to the pups.

Weeks six and seven are also a good time to introduce more new experiences–the vacuum cleaner, blow dryer, short car rides, and carefully screened visitors, human as well as gentle adult dogs that the breeder has. Short training sessions are very productive at this time and prepare pups for later training.

Puppy's First Exam

You should schedule a veterinary examination for your new puppy within 72 hours of bringing him home. In fact, most breeders require that you have the pup examined within a certain time frame to validate their health guarantees. This initial examination will confirm that your puppy's in good health and establish some baselines for future reference.

At this first examination, your vet will check your pup's overall health and condition. She will weigh him and determine the health of his skin and coat, which can be indicators of general health and well-being. She will listen to his heart and lungs and check his ears, gums, bite, and external eye area. Many young puppies have round worms, even when they come from responsible breeders, so be sure to provide a fecal sample for your vet to check.

You might ask your vet to check your puppy's patellas (knee caps), which she can do through simple manipulation, to be sure they don't luxate (slip).

Vaccines are often given at this first exam as well. Be sure to give your veterinarian whatever vaccination and other health records your breeder has provided.

If you live in an area in which heartworm is a concern, you will want to start your puppy on heartworm prevention at this first visit (or continue it if your breeder started him). The dosage of heartworm preventative is determined by the dog's weight, so you'll need to have your puppy reweighed every month to determine the right dosage until he is fully grown.

Puppy Vaccinations

Your Labrador puppy–just like his human companions–is most susceptible to infectious diseases during the first months of his life. If a bitch was properly vaccinated before she was bred, her newborn puppies will receive immunities against many diseases from the colostrum contained in her first milk. During the first 24 hours after birth, the puppies' intestinal walls are very thin, allowing antigens (which provide passive immunity) from the colostrum to pass to the puppies. Colostrum is present for only about 24 hours after whelping and no antigens are passed to the puppies after that time, so it's vital that puppies nurse soon after birth. Puppies that do not are more vulnerable to disease than pups that do.

A puppy's immunity from colostrum protects him for only his first few weeks. Your puppy needs to be vaccinated to stimulate his immune system to build antibodies. Most vaccines are administered by injection subcutaneously (under the skin) or intramuscularly (into the muscle), but a few are given by nasal spray. It's impossible to determine when the immunity from the colostrum is gone, so puppies have traditionally been given a series of vaccinations beginning at five to six weeks and repeating every two to four weeks through three or four sets.

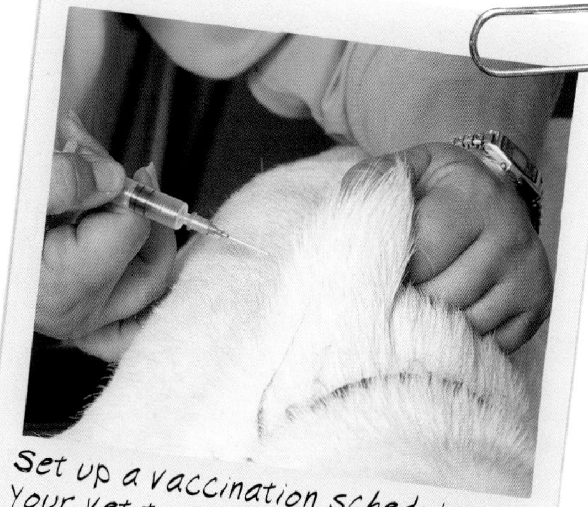

Set up a vaccination schedule with your vet to make sure your dog is protected properly.

Many veterinarians now delay the first round of vaccinations until eight weeks or later. The American Veterinary Medical Association (AVMA) and several veterinary have recently changed their recommended vaccination schedules. Ask your veterinarian about an appropriate schedule for you puppy. Dogs are commonly vaccinated against some or all of the following diseases.

Rabies

Rabies is a viral disease that attacks the central nervous system of any warm-blooded animal, including people. Rabies is spread in the saliva of an infected animal, usually through a bite. Wild animals, including skunks, foxes, raccoons, coyotes, and bats, are commonly infected with rabies and can pass the disease to domestic animals, who can in turn pass it to people.

Rabies takes two forms in its victims. The furious form is what most of us imagine as the "mad" behavior of a rabid animal, including aggression and foaming at the mouth. In dumb rabies, the animal becomes paralyzed, usually starting with the lower jaw and moving through the limbs and vital organs until death occurs.

Some diseases are transmitted by other animals, especially other dogs.

Rabies is always fatal once symptoms appear. State laws throughout the US require that dogs and cats be vaccinated against rabies, every year in some states and every three years in others. Your puppy should have his initial rabies vaccination when he is three to four months old. Rabies is one of only a few diseases that dogs can transmit to people. Because the disease is so deadly, it's essential that you keep your pets' rabies vaccinations up to date.

Canine Distemper

Canine Distemper is a highly contagious viral disease. Early symptoms include respiratory problems, and sometimes vomiting and diarrhea. Distemper may also affect the nervous system. Most of the puppies and about half of the adult dogs that contract canine distemper die from the disease. Survivors often suffer partial or total paralysis and/or loss of vision, hearing, and sense of smell. Vaccination for distemper involves a series of four initial injections, and follow-up boosters as recommended by your vet, usually annually.

Infectious Canine Hepatitis

Infectious Canine Hepatitis is viral disease that attacks many tissues. The liver is usually the most seriously damaged. The virus is spread in the urine of infected dogs. Vaccinations are usually given in a series of three shots.

Canine Parvovirus

Canine Parvovirus (CPV), or "parvo," is an extremely contagious and deadly viral disease. The virus can survive exposure to extreme temperatures and most disinfectants, so it is very difficult to kill. Parvo is spread in the feces of infected dogs. It can be picked up and carried on shoes, paws, and clothing and spread from one place to another. Parvo contamination can last for extended periods.

Parvovirus affects the intestinal tract, heart muscle, and white blood cells. Symptoms include vomiting, severe diarrhea with a distinctive foul odor, depression, high fever, and loss of appetite. Infected dogs often die within two to three days after symptoms appear. In puppies under three months old, parvo can cause myocarditis (inflammation of the heart), and puppies that survive usually have permanent heart damage. Parvo vaccines are given to puppies in a series of three, followed by boosters for adult dogs.

Canine Bordatellosis

Canine Bordatellosis, also known as "Bordatella" or "kennel cough," is a bacterial disease of the respiratory tract. The primary symptom is a cough that makes your Lab sound like an elephant seal. A dog with Bordatella may also have a runny nose. Kennel cough isn't very serious in a healthy adult, but it can kill a puppy. Vaccines are usually given by nasal spray, but injectable vaccines are also available. Vaccination schedules for Bordatella vary, so ask your veterinarian.

Canine Parainfluenza

Canine Parainfluenza is a viral disease that causes respiratory tract infection. Puppy vaccinations are usually given in a series of three, usually with other vaccines for broader protection.

Canine Leptospirosis

Canine Leptospirosis, or "Lepto," is a bacterial disease that attacks the kidney and can cause kidney failure. Symptoms include vomiting, convulsions, and vision problems. Lepto is spread in the urine of infected animals. It's not very common in most areas and different strains occur. The vaccine has little effect on the most common strain of Lepto, and there is a relatively high incidence of reaction to the vaccine, so many breeders and owners do not vaccinate against Lepto. Ask your veterinarian about your dog's risk of exposure before vaccinating him. If vaccination for Lepto seems appropriate in you circumstances, consider giving the vaccine at a different time from the others to control negative reactions.

Other Canine Diseases

Other canine diseases occur in some areas. Ask your vet about your dog's risk of exposure to Coronavirus, Lyme disease, and other diseases. There is no reason to vaccinate your dog against diseases that pose no risk for him, but you probably don't want to leave him vulnerable to something that's a problem where you live or travel.

General Schedule for Puppy Vaccinations

The following schedule is intended only as a guideline. Your puppy may not need all the vaccines listed, or your vet may recommend some that are not listed, depending on your puppy's risk of exposure to various diseases. Discuss the specific vaccinations and schedule with your veterinarian.

Disease	First Vaccination	Second Vaccination	Third Vaccination
Distemper	6-10	10-12	14-16
Infectious canine hepatitis	6-8	10-12	14-16
Parvovirus infection	6-8	10-12	14-16
Bordatellosis	6-8	0-12	14-16
Parainfluenza	6-8	10-12	14-16
Leptospirosis (if given)	10-12	14-16	
Rabies	12		

Teething

Puppies start to lose their baby (deciduous) teeth and get their permanent teeth when they're four or five months of age. The small front incisors will come out first, then the premolars, which are right behind the canine teeth, then the big back molars, and finally the canine teeth. Teething usually goes smoothly, other than some discomfort and bleeding gums, but check your puppy's mouth every few days. If your puppy retains a baby tooth when the adult tooth is coming in your vet may need to pull the baby tooth.

Your puppy's mouth may be sore while he's teething, and he'll probably want to chew a lot. Here are some things you can do to keep him more comfortable:

• Give him an ice cube or a "soupsicle" made by freezing low-sodium chicken or beef broth into ice cubes.

• Soak a clean, old washcloth or small towel in water, wring it out, roll it up, and freeze it. Give it to your puppy to chew, but only when you're with him. Puppies have been known to swallow towels.

• Give him Nylabone® chew toys.

• Give him a raw carrot.

• If you feed him dry food, soak it in water for about 20 minutes to soften it before feeding him.

• Crate or confine him when you can't watch him, and keep anything you don't want him to chew out of his reach

Puppies need things to chew on to promote proper tooth development.

Health Care for the Adolescent Lab

Adolescent Labs are cute as the dickens, many of them in a rather goofy sort of way. Like their human counterparts, they go through several awkward periods as various parts grow faster than others. At about four or five months, your cute, round puppy will be replaced by a rather skinny, leggy creature with ears too big for his head. He'll stay that way for several months. At seven to nine months, he may appear to be running down hill, as his hind legs grow longer than his front ones. Fear not! Enjoy your puppy's silly puppyhood–he'll outgrow the awkwardness and lack of proportion. By two years of age, most Labs have finished growing. They may still need to fill out a bit as they mature further, but they have their height. So if your cute little puppy turns into a silly looking "teenager," relax–a beautiful dog is in the making.

Vaccinations

If your puppy was properly vaccinated during his first 4 to 6 months, his next set of vaccinations will be due when he is about 16 months old, if your veterinarian follows a traditional vaccination schedule. In other words, about a year after your pup receives his final puppy shots, your vet will recommend booster shots for distemper, infectious canine hepatitis, parvovirus, and parainfluenza. Depending on where you live and your dog's risk of exposure, your vet may also recommend boosters for leptospirosis, bordatella (kennel cough), coronavirus, and Lyme disease. Boosters for rabies are required every year or every three years, depending on state law.

Vaccinations are a subject of considerable controversy. There is evidence that excessive vaccination is both unnecessary and potentially harmful to the animal's immune system. Some vets are now using antibody titres rather than routine vaccinations. A titre is a test on a sample of blood that measures the level of immunity to a particular disease. Other vets are using new protocols put forth by various veterinary colleges. Colorado State University, for instance, now recommends booster vaccinations one year after the standard three-shot puppy series, and then every three years (except rabies, which depends on state laws). You may want to discuss the new recommendations with your veterinarian.

Annual trips to the vet for exams and booster shots will help keep your Lab healthy.

External Parasite Control

Young Labs are very active and love to run and play outdoors. Unfortunately, there are some nasty little critters that will latch onto your dog, and they'll stay there if you let them. Let's see who they are and what you can do about them.

Antibody Titres

An antibody titre is a blood test used to determine antibody levels in an animal's blood. Some dog owners and veterinarians prefer to do titres before re-vaccinating to avoid over-vaccinating the dog. Other vets feel titres are meaningless as indicators of the need for booster shots because laboratory results have been shown to be wildly inconsistent and because titres don't necessarily give an accurate assessment of immunity—a dog may have a low titre and still be protected against a particular disease.

Insects and other external parasites can irritate your Lab's skin.

Fleas

Fleas are tiny little red, black, or brown insects. Adult fleas suck the blood of a host animal, while flea larvae feed on the adult fleas' feces, which is rich in blood. You can sometimes see flea "dirt" on the skin of a dog with fleas. It looks like tiny clusters of blackish specks, rather like black pepper. If you wet flea dirt slightly, it turns red because it's made up mainly of blood. Fleas sometimes lay their eggs on the host animal, but usually they lay them on the host's bedding, carpets, and other favorable places. Flea eggs usually hatch in 4 to 21 days, depending on the temperature, but they can survive up to 18 months. Flea larva look like tiny maggots. The larvae molts twice and then forms a pupae, from which an adult flea will eventually emerge. Flea pupae can survive long periods until the temperature, or the vibration of a nearby host, causes the fleas inside them to emerge.

Fleas are annoying little monsters. Worse, they carry tapeworm and disease. If they infest a host in large numbers, they can cause anemia. If your dog is allergic to flea saliva and is bitten by a flea, he'll scratch and bite himself raw. So watch out for fleas! Ask your vet about flea-control strategies that will work best for your situation and area.

Examine your dog carefully during tick season and ask your vet about the risk of

Benefits of Grooming

Grooming isn't just to make your Lab look beautiful. Daily brushing will give you time to inspect your dog's skin for parasites or any other problems there might be.

Ticks

Ticks are arthropods, or relatives of spiders. They have eight legs and most are round and flat unless they are gorged with blood or gravid with eggs, when they look like beans with little legs. Dogs often pick up ticks in brushy fields, but other animals or birds can deposit ticks just about anywhere, including your own yard. In order to feed, the tick buries its head parts in the host animal and gorges on blood. Like fleas, ticks carry disease.

The deer tick, which spreads Lyme disease that can cripple a dog (or a person), is very small and difficult to find, especially in dog fur. By the time a deer tick is big enough to see easily, it may have been feeding on the dog for several days and may already have transmitted Lyme disease to the dog. Ask your veterinarian about the risk of Lyme where you live. If you walk your dog in an area that may harbor deer ticks, go over him with a fine-toothed flea comb at least once a day. If your dog seems sluggish or sore, take him to your vet.

Ticks must be removed carefully. If you pull the body off and leave the head in the skin, it may become infected. It's also important not to squeeze a tick when removing it, as that can force infectious fluids from the tick into the host. You can find special tick-removers in some pet-supply stores. Or you can dab the tick with strong saline solution, iodine, or alcohol to make it loosen its grip, and then pull it gently out with forceps, tweezers, or your fingers with a tissue over the tick. Don't twist–pull straight out so that the head will come with the body. Dispose of the tick, preferably by flushing it down the toilet. Check the dog's skin. You should see a small hole where the tick bit into the skin. If you see a black spot, you've left the head. If that happens, keep an eye on the spot for several days in case it becomes infected. After you remove the tick, clean the bite with alcohol, Betadine, or iodine, let it dry, and apply antiseptic ointment. Wash your hands and any tool you used. If ticks are common in your area, ask your vet about a suitable means of control.

Other Skin Problems

Ringworm

Ringworm is a highly contagious fungal infection, not a worm. It usually shows up as a sore-looking bald circle, but if you find any bald patches on your dog, have your veterinarian check him. Don't waste time with home remedies–fungal infections are difficult to treat and more difficult to cure. Dispose of all bedding your dog has used, preferably by burning. Ringworm can spread to your other pets, and to people, so if you suspect ringworm, take you dog to the vet immediately. If your dog does have ringworm, ask your vet how to keep it from spreading in your household.

Mange

Mange is caused by several species of mites that eat skin debris, hair follicles, and tissue. Symptoms of mange include hair loss followed by flaky, crusty skin. Often dogs will scratch themselves and make the original condition worse by creating sores that are vulnerable to viral, fungal, or parasitic infection. If you think that your dog may have mange, have him examined by your vet. To treat mange effectively, it's essential to determine the species of mite causing the problem.

A dog that scratches a lot may have something irritating his skin.

Eczema

Eczema refers to a multitude of skin problems with diverse causes. Sunburn, chemicals, food allergies, drugs, pollen, stress and other things can cause itching, hair loss, and open sores. It's often difficult to determine the cause of eczema, which makes effective treatment difficult. Once again, it is important to work closely with your veterinarian to diagnose and cure eczema.

Intestinal Worms

There are many species of parasitic worms, and a number of them can infest dogs and other animals. Some worms cause no problems and you never know they exist. Others are tolerated in small numbers, but cause major problems in larger numbers. Puppies should have fecal exams when they get their vaccinations, and adult dogs should have fecal exams at least once a year. If you see evidence of worms in your dog's stools, take a specimen to your vet so that he can identify the worm and prescribe an effective treatment.

Roundworms

Roundworms look like spaghetti and can grow to a length of 8 inches (20 cm). They eat digesting food in the host's intestines. A puppy with chronic roundworm infection is often thin with a pot-belly. He may vomit and have diarrhea. For a while, he'll be hungry all the time, but eventually he'll stop eating. Roundworms are common in puppies, even those that come from clean surroundings, and responsible breeders have their bitches and puppies checked regularly and wormed when necessary to eliminate the worms. Roundworms can be passed to people, so until your puppy is pronounced free of worms by your veterinarian, practice proper hygiene and teach children to do the same.

Tapeworms

Tapeworms are hard to diagnose from fecal specimens, but the worms shed segments, which look like rice and can be found sticking to the area around the anus. Dogs get tapeworms by eating mice, fleas, rabbits, and other animals that serve as intermediate hosts while the worms are in the larval stage. The worms then develop in the dog. If you keep your dog free of fleas, he's less likely to get tapeworm.

Other Worms

Puppies and dogs can also get hookworms, whipworms, and threadworms, which can cause a variety of problems including diarrhea, weight loss, anemia, and respiratory infection

Your dog's best protections against worms are a clean environment, your attention to telltale symptoms, and regular veterinary and fecal examinations.

Heartworm

Heartworm is a horrible parasite that takes up residence in the heart and, left untreated, eventually kills the dog. Heartworm larva are carried by a mosquito from an infected dog to a new host. The larva then travel to the host's heart, where they take up residence, mature into worms, and grow. Eventually they fill the heart and cause congestive heart failure. Luckily, heartworm is easy to prevent with daily or monthly preventive medication. As an added bonus, many heartworm preventatives also prevent intestinal worms.

Heartworm disease occurs in some areas and not in others. Ask your veterinarian about the need for heartworm tests and prevention where you live. If you plan to travel with your dog, check before you go–your dog may need protection during your travels.

Sex and the Single Lab

Adolescence is a time of many changes in your Lab. Your dog will become sexually mature and experience hormonal changes that will affect his or her behavior. This is the time to have your Lab spayed or neutered. But you may want to breed your Lab, you say? Okay, let's take a quick look at the realities of dog breeding.

Breeding—or Not!

You love your Lab and have several friends who "want one of her puppies." You think it would be fun to have a litter, and maybe you could even make some money. Besides, what better way for the kids to learn about "the miracle of birth?" Before you take the leap and breed your Lab, please consider the following points, and reread chapters two and three. Then, if you want to breed, contact an experienced breeder or two, get some guidance, and please, do it responsibly.

Before being bred, the perspective dam and sire should be cleared for any genetic diseases.

Before she is considered for breeding, a Labrador bitch needs at minimum to have her hips and elbows x-rayed and certified free from hip and elbow dysplasia by OFA, PennHIP, and/or Wind-Morgan. Re-member, no one can tell whether your dog has dysplasia by watching the dog move.

A lot of time and energy go into raising a healthy litter of puppies.

Some people claim that they can–don't buy into that. Even board certified veterinary orthopedic specialists can't do that! If your Lab is dysplastic, or carries the genes for dysplasia, some or all of her puppies could be crippled as adults. That's not a nice thing for the affected dog or for the person who gets the dog from you. Believe me, I know–I have a Lab with hip and elbow dysplasia. She's a wonderful dog, but she cost a fortune in vet bills and she went through over a year of serious pain and limping. Her breeder, I found out later, has produced lots of dogs–her relatives–with hip and elbow problems. You don't really want to put puppies and people through that, do you? Your Lab bitch should also have her eyes cleared annually by a veterinary ophthalmologist, and preferably have her heart certified healthy. Problems in any of these areas can be passed to the puppies from the mother, father, or both.

Testing for genetic disease is expensive, but without it, you run the risk of producing puppies with serious problems. Besides, responsible, well-informed buyers who would give your puppies the kind of homes they deserve won't buy from a breeder who doesn't do the proper tests.

A knowledgeable person should also evaluate your bitch to assess her strengths and weaknesses in terms of the breed standard so that you can choose a stud dog that will complement your bitch–he should be strong where she is weak and vice versa so that you don't reproduce the weaknesses in either parent. No dog is perfect, of course, but responsible breeders try to improve the dogs they produce with every generation. Even if all your puppies will go to pet homes, I'm sure you want them to be healthy, handsome Labs their owners can live with and be proud of.

If you still think you want to breed, then it's time to face some more serious issues. Getting a bitch through a healthy pregnancy, and then managing a litter of 8 to 12 (or more!) lively puppies for at least 7 weeks, isn't all fun and games. There's nothing cuter than a Labrador puppy, that's for sure. But there's a lot more to babies of any species than cuteness. You will have to provide a safe place for your puppies to play, eat, and sleep. You'll have to provide their dam with lots of food while she's nursing, and then provide the puppies with lots more food from about the fourth week on. You'll have to provide toys, veterinary care, vaccinations, fecal exams, and worming. Puppies also need a tireless maid. Believe me, they pee and poop a lot, tear things up, spill their food and water, break things, vomit, and occasionally get hurt. They do look like little angels when they're asleep.

Healthy pups are the result of extensive planning and care.

Canine pregnancies, like human pregnancies, don't always go well. Labs in general carry their litters easily and are "free whelpers," meaning they give birth on their own with few problems for the most part. But not always. Pregnancy sometimes brings on gestational diabetes, which can threaten the lives of both the mother and the pups. Pregnancies are sometimes lost entirely through reabsorption or spontaneous abortion (miscarriage). There are other risks as well.

If you're doing this so that your kids can witness the miracle of birth, be forewarned that few bitches whelp on schedule. Will your children sit up with a panting, pacing, paper-shredding bitch for 36 hours while she decides whether it's *really* time? Will you? What if she has her puppies when you're not home? What if she has them on your new couch (happened to me!) or your bed?

As in any birth, things can and sometimes do go terribly wrong. Are you prepared to take your bitch to an emergency vet at 2 a.m. for a costly caesarian section? Bitches and puppies sometimes die during or shortly after whelping. Is this experience worth the risk of losing your beloved pet? Puppies, just like children, can be born with serious birth defects, ranging from cleft palates that prevent them from nursing properly to hydrocephalus (water on the brain) to missing or deformed organs to autoimmune diseases. Are you prepared to deal with such puppies? Even with careful planning, proper equipment, and the best of care, puppies sometimes simply do not make it. Are you and your family prepared for the

The Cost of Breeding a Litter

What does it cost to breed a litter responsibly? Here's a run-down of the approximate minimum cost of responsibly breeding a litter:

Equipment

Whelping box—$100

Whelping box heating pad—$70

Weight scale—$40

Indoor puppy pen—$100

First aid and emergency supplies—$40

Total minimum for equipment = $350

Veterinary Clearances for Female Prior to Breeding

X-rays and certifications for hip and elbow dysplasia—$200

Heart certification by a board certified cardiologist—$150

Eye certifications by board certified veterinary ophthalmologist—$30

Pre-breeding examination of female (check for intestinal parasites, brucellosis test, booster immunizations, pelvic exam, and health certificate—$150

Transportation to veterinarians for exams—varies

Total—$520+ (does not include purchase price of breeding-quality bitch, nor training and showing her to titles)

Breeding and Pre-natal Expenses

Average stud fee—$600

Extra food and vitamins for female when in whelp—$150

Transportation to the Stud Dog—varies

Total minimum for breeding—$750

Whelping Expenses

Bedding—$40

Cleaning supplies—$20

Total minimum for whelping (barring emergencies)—$100

C-section if necessary—$800

Postpartum Expenses for a Litter of Eight

Postpartum check for female—$50

Examination of litter—$50

Removal of dewclaws at $10 per puppy—$80

Puppy immunizations at $40 per puppy (assuming 2 sets each—add more if pups are not sold by 10-12 weeks of age)—$320

Food for puppies before and after weaning—$200+

Worming at least twice—$50

Advertising the litter—$150

Total minimum postpartum expenses—$900

Total minimum expenses—$2620 (Note: this does not include toys, collars, leashes, and crates for puppies, laundry expenses, cost of extra electricity for whelping room, cost of replacing lawn, woodwork, or whatever pups may damage— or many other expenses!)

Value of your Time

You won't get paid for the time you spend, but time does have economic value—not to mention that the time you spend caring for a litter is time you are unable to give to other interests, your family, your children, or yourself. Breeders go very short on sleep when they have puppies! This is a very conservative estimate of the time it takes to raise a litter properly.

Planning the breeding—40 hours

Transporting the bitch to the stud and breeding—10 to 25 hours

Setting up whelping area—4 hours

Monitoring labor and whelping time—24 hours

Time spent with puppies and cleaning up after puppies—5 hours/day = 35 hrs/week x 9 weeks = 315 hours

Transporting puppies to the vet for postnatal exam, and two sets of shots—12 hours

Time answering phone calls and mail about puppies—1 hour/day = 7 hours/week x 9 weeks = 63 hours

Total minimum time = 479 hours = 26+ hours per week for 9 weeks of pregnancy and 9 weeks of puppies

Assuming you can sell each puppy for $500, that you have only the minimum expenses outlined above, and that your time expenditure is also the minimum described above, you will work very hard for 18 weeks for $3.92 an hour. That's optimistic! So if you want to make money, get a job or start a real business.

Part 2

heartbreak of having a beautiful puppy stillborn or watching it die in your hands? These things don't happen all the time, of course. But no one should breed a litter without being prepared for the worst, because the worst can happen. It's happened to me.

But let's assume all goes perfectly, and you have a reasonable Labrador litter of eight. What if those people who wanted one of your puppies change their minds when the time comes? What if you only have homes for four? You are responsible for the lives of all your puppies because you decided they should be born. Are you willing to take care of every single puppy that doesn't have a home for as long as necessary? What if someone no longer wants one of them four or five years from now? Are you willing to take back any pups whose new homes don't work out for whatever reason? As I write this I have in my house a dog that was born into my hands, sold to a family as a pet, and returned to me at four years of age because they were moving and didn't want him any more. It happens.

Please spay or neuter your pet.

Many dedicated, responsible breeders find the satisfaction of breeding quality dogs worth the risks, hard work, pain, and sorrow. But don't kid yourself–done right, raising puppies isn't just cuddling little furballs and smelling puppy breath. It's also a lot of hard physical work. It involves lots of messes, and it takes a lot of your time for at least two months. It's expensive. Sometimes it's heartbreaking. And if it's done carelessly, it's the dogs and their buyers who suffer most.

Spaying and Neutering

The Labrador Retriever Club of America strongly recommends that you have your pet Lab spayed or neutered. Most responsible breeders require this by selling their pet puppies with spay/neuter contracts and limited registration, which means that while the puppy itself is registered, any offspring it may produce through irresponsible breeding will not be eligible for registration.

Why the emphasis on spaying and neutering? First, visit your local animal shelter or call your local Lab rescue volunteer. Before you even think of breeding your dog, you need to be aware that many, many Labs are produced and discarded every year.

There are also very good health reasons to alter your pet Lab. Sexually intact dogs of both sexes are at a greater risk of cancer. Spaying your female puppy will prevent her ever developing uterine infections or cancer and will reduce her risk of mammary tumors. Spaying also eliminates the mess of a heat cycle every six months and safeguards your pet Lab from the risks of pregnancy and whelping.

Please don't breed your bitch just once to calm her down. That old idea is just not true. Obedience training, proper exercise, and maturity, not motherhood, lead to calmer behavior in young Labs. Having a litter won't improve your bitch's personality, either. If anything, having puppies will take her focus away from her human family.

Neutering your male Lab will eliminate his risk of testicular cancer and greatly reduce his risk of developing prostate problems. It will likely improve his attitude, too, as neutered males tend to be more tolerant of other male dogs, and less interested in roaming.

Spaying or neutering will not change your Lab's basic personality and won't cause obesity, which comes from too much food and too little exercise.

Health Care for the Prime of Life

You've made it through the first two raucous years of your Labrador's life–hurrah! You're dog is entering the prime years of young adulthood. If you've done right by him in terms of training, socialization, exercise, nutrition, and health care, he is maturing into a fine, sensible companion, and your relationship can only get better over the next few years. Maintaining your Lab in good health through his prime years will contribute to his ability to fulfill his role as a terrific companion and will increase the chances that he'll remain healthy into old age.

Health care is, of course, of life-long importance to dogs as it is to people. Your Lab should see his veterinarian at least once a year, even if he appears to be healthy. Regular examinations can reveal problems early on, and preventive care will help keep him healthy and prevent some problems common to Labs or to dogs in general. Routine care and grooming can go a long way to keeping your Labrador's teeth and gums, ears, and skin healthy.

Vital Signs

Here are the normal ranges for a dog's temperature, pulse, and breathing rate:

√ Temperature: 99.5°F-102.8°F

√ Pulse: 60-120 beats per minute

√ Breathing: 14-22 breaths per minute

Jumping from a high place can injure your Lab pup's joints.

Regular Examinations

Your Lab should see the veterinarian at least once a year for a routine examination. Even if he's on a reduced vaccination schedule, take him in for an annual checkup. Early detection of health problems can mean the difference between a quick, relatively easy cure and long-term, chronic problems in many cases.

Special Labrador Health Issues

In addition to the inherited diseases discussed earlier, some Labrador Retrievers develop some of the following health problems. Don't panic! Most Labs remain healthy throughout their lives. On the other hand, good and bad health are facts of life for dogs as well as for people, and being well informed is always an advantage.

Cruciate Ligament Injuries

Many young Labs suffer cruciate ligament injuries. While this is not an inherited condition, Labs do seem prone to these injuries, which occur when the rear legs are twisted during strenuous activity (for instance, jumping to catch an object in mid-air). Mild cases may resolve themselves with rest, but treatment usually involves surgery followed by extremely restricted activity, often for several months.

Cold Tail

Cold tail (also called wash tail or limber tail) is a condition in which the dog's tail goes limp. It appears to be brought on by swimming in cold water, which may cause a muscle spasm or glandular reaction of some sort. Cold tail is not a serious problem, and should go away within a few days without treatment.

Heart Disease

A heart defect called Tricuspid Valve Dysplasia (TVD) has recently been identified in Labrador Retrievers. After a stud dog on the west coast produced a number of puppies that died young of TVD, he was tested by echocardiogram and found to have a very mild case.

Very little is known at this time about the prevalence of TVD in Labs or about how it is inherited. In mild cases, an auscultation (examination by stethoscope) will not diagnose the problem, so ask the breeder about heart problems in her lines and whether her breeding dogs have been screened and cleared by echocardiogram. Since not many Labs have yet been cleared, ask about longevity and incidence of heart disease in the lines you consider.

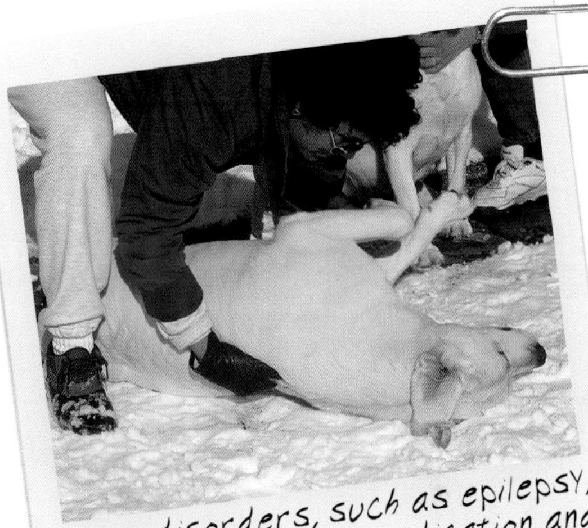

Some disorders, such as epilepsy, can be treated with medication and help your Lab live a normal life.

Epilepsy

Epilepsy is a seizure disorder that occurs in Labrador Retrievers and other breeds. Epilepsy cannot be cured, but it can be controlled in most cases with medication. Most epileptic dogs can live fairly normal lives, but under no circumstances should a dog with epilepsy be bred. Ask breeders about epilepsy in their dogs' bloodlines. Keep in mind as well that many things, including physical trauma to the head, chemical agents, heat stroke, and other factors, can cause seizures in dogs. Not all seizures are inherited, and the presence of a single dog with seizures shouldn't be taken as evidence of inherited epilepsy in the line. On the other hand, several relatives with seizures should be a red light.

Health Care for the Senior Lab

When will your Labrador Retriever become a senior citizen? Dogs age differently, but if your Lab comes from reasonably healthy, long-lived family lines, and if you have provided him with good health care, exercise, and nutrition throughout his life, he should still be going pretty strong at nine or ten years of age, although some well-cared-for Labs do begin to show the effects of aging a bit earlier than that.

Routine care and exercise will keep your older Lab fit and healthy.

Relaxing in his favorite spot on the couch makes the author's senior Lab happy.

Even if he appears to be in the prime of health, speak to your vet about recommended changes in health care that may stave off problems as the gray around that lovely Labrador muzzle increases. In general, when your Lab is between six and eight years old, you should begin thinking about signs of aging and what they mean and ask your vet about early screening for age-related problems. Geriatric screening will depend in part on your dog's health history and may include blood tests, x-rays, or an electrocardiogram. You can help your vet by scheduling a visit if you notice that your dog experiences a sudden loss of weight or appetite, increase in appetite without weight gain, increased thirst, diarrhea or vomiting lasting more than a day, coughing, or excessive panting.

One of the first signs of advancing age is a general slowing down. Your once rambunctious Lab does things more slowly and deliberately. His hearing and vision may not be as good as when he was younger, and he may be losing muscle tone and getting a bit creaky. Regardless of your dog's age, it may be worth having your vet give him a thorough exam if you notice these changes.

Routine Health Care

Aside from being sure your aging Lab gets a checkup at least annually, and other veterinary care as needed, there are some things you can do on a routine basis to keep him healthy and to catch problems early on.

Arthritis, thyroid imbalance, excess weight, and other conditions can cause symptoms similar to aging, and treatment may give your dog several more good years.

Behavioral changes also occur in some aging dogs. Your dog may become anxious when you aren't with him or become sensitive to noises such as thunder that never bothered him much before. He may seem confused or disoriented at times and may begin to have elimination problems. If you notice any of these changes, see your vet. Some of them may simply be due to aging, but some may be treatable.

Vaccinations

Speak to your veterinarian about your senior Lab's need for vaccinations. Many vets feel that older dogs should be vaccinated less frequently than younger ones, if at all, because they are already adequately protected against disease, and excessive vaccination can compromise the immune system, leading to illness.

Special Health Issues for Older Labrador Retrievers

Laryngeal Paralysis

Laryngeal paralysis is a condition in which one or both sides of the larynx fail to open and close properly. In severe cases, the dog will be unable to get sufficient oxygen. He may also overheat because he can no longer pant effectively. Rough, noisy breathing and a change in the dog's bark are early signs of laryngeal paralysis. In Labrador Retrievers, laryngeal paralysis occurs primarily in old age.

Accurate diagnosis is difficult, and not all vets are experienced with the condition, so ask for a referral to a specialist or a vet more familiar with the condition if yours is not. Treatment for laryngeal paralysis involves tacking open one or more of the laryngeal folds, enabling the dog to breathe properly. The downside of the treatment is that the dog is susceptible to aspiration pneumonia, although that can be controlled for the most part by elevating food bowls and prohibiting swimming. Many Labs with laryngeal paralysis also do fine for quite a while with no treatment but close monitoring, especially in hot weather. The severity of the problem, and your dog's age and general health, will be factors to discuss with your vet if your dog develops the condition.

Mental Health

Your elderly Lab will probably sleep more than he used to. He may not ask you to go play ball as often as he did a few years ago. He may seem content to just lie in the corner a lot of the time. But don't forget that he still needs your attention and affection and can become depressed and lonely without it. A short walk once or twice a day can boost his spirits, and a cuddle and belly rub will certainly be welcomed by most aging Labs.

Potential Orthopedic Problems in Labs

Serious and debilitating problems in the hip, elbow, shoulder, and hock joints have become far too common in Labs over the past two decades. This is due in part to the increased popularity of the breed, which in turn has led some irresponsible people to produce Lab

Proper nutrition, weight control, and exercise can help prevent symptoms of some orthopedic problems.

Part 2

puppies just to make money, or for other haphazard reasons, with no thought to careful selection of genetically healthy animals for breeding. Joint problems cannot always be detected simply by watching a dog move, especially if the dog is young and reasonably fit. Lameness may be subtle and difficult to detect, or the dog may be affected equally on both sides. In other words, a dog may not appear to be lame, but may in fact have an orthopedic problem that may be passed to its offspring. At present, radiography (x-rays) is the best method for diagnosing the following genetically transmitted orthopedic problems.

At two years of age, your Lab becomes eligible for a hip and elbow certifications from the Orthopedic Foundation for Animals (OFA). Hopefully, his parents and their relatives had certificates vouching for their orthopedic health before you took your puppy home. In any case, there are good reasons to consider having your Lab's hips and elbows x-rayed under the protocol of the OFA, PennHIP, or Wind-Morgan program.

Even if your Lab is simply a pet, and his athletic pursuits are limited to walks around the block and games of fetch-the-ball in the backyard, it may be an advantage to have him x-rayed. If he shows the potential for arthritis due to poorly formed joints, you will be able to put him on preventive care with the help of your veterinarian. Early intervention in the form of nutritional support, weight control, and proper exercise can go a long way to preventing orthopedic problems even if your dog has a genetic predisposition for them.

If your dog is active in canine sports, it's a good idea to be sure he's structurally sound. Jumping and other strenuous activity can be devastating to a dog with joint problems. Of course, if you want to use your Lab for breeding, you must have him or her cleared by one or more of the orthopedic registries if you want to be an ethical breeder.

Canine Hip Dysplasia

Canine hip dysplasia, or CHD, is a serious, potentially crippling, condition in which the bones that make up the hip joint are malformed and do not fit together properly. This poor

Organizations Evaluating Orthopedic Health in Dogs

OFA

The Orthopedic Foundation for Animals (OFA) rates the structure of hips by evaluating x-rays. To be certified, the dog must be at least 24 months old when x-rayed. Dogs that are considered free of Canine hip dysplasia (CHD) are rated Excellent, Good, or Fair. Dysplasia is also ranked at three levels of severity. Preliminary OFA evaluations can be made at one year of age.

PennHIP

The Pennsylvania Hip Improvement Program (PennHIP) also uses x-rays to evaluate hip structure, but their method for doing so is different from that used by OFA, and puppies as young as four months can be checked for hip laxity that may lead to the arthritic changes typical of hip dysplasia.

Wind-Morgan Program

The Wind-Morgan Program collects data on heritable diseases of the hip, shoulder, elbow, and hock joints in Labrador Retrievers. The elbows, shoulders, and hocks can usually be evaluated accurately when the dog is 12 months old, and a preliminary evaluation of the hip joint can be made at the same time. Preliminary evaluations of the elbows, shoulders, hocks, and hips can be made when the pup is six months old. Dogs showing signs of lameness can be evaluated at any age. The Wind-Morgan database provides an excellent tool for reducing the incidence of orthopedic disease in Labs, and should be utilized by breeders and buyers alike.

Outside the United States

Other methods of evaluation are used in Canada, Britain, and other parts of the world. Check with your veterinarian for the appropriate rating system.

fit makes the dog prone to development of painful arthritis, often beginning as young as four or five months. CHD is inherited and cannot be diagnosed or ruled out just by watching a dog move. All Labs used for breeding should be x-rayed and the x-rays should be evaluated by experts at the Orthopedic Foundation for Animals (OFA), Penn-HIP, and/or Wind-Morgan programs in the US or the appropriate equivalent program elsewhere.

Some dogs with CHD never show clinical symptoms, but if their x-rays show evidence of dysplasia, they should not be used for breeding.

Elbow Dysplasia

Elbow dysplasia is a general term used to identify inherited elbow disease in dogs. Elbow dysplasia can consist of one or any combination of the following conditions: fragmented medial coronoid of the ulna, osteochondritis of the medial humeral condyle in the elbow joint, and ununited anconeal process. All those terms essentially mean that the formation of the elbow joint is abnormal.

Symptoms of elbow dysplasia include lameness and faulty gait in which the front toes turn inward as the dog attempts to compensate for pain in the elbow. Range of motion of the elbow is usually restricted as well. Elbow dysplasia is often bilateral, occurring in both elbows. The age at which elbow dysplasia becomes apparent varies depending on the specific genes the individual inherits as well as environmental factors such as weight and exercise.

Osteochondrosis

The heads of a dog's long leg bones are protected by a cushion of cartilage at the joints. The cartilage protects the bone but is itself prone to injury, especially in a large, active young dog. In ostcochondrosis (OC), the cartilage within one or more joints cracks and tears. If pieces of cartilage break free and float in and near a joint, the condition is known as osteochondrosis dissecans (OCD). Inflammation of the joint (arthritis), pain, and lameness usually result.

OCD most commonly affects the shoulder or elbow but may also occur in the hip, the knee, or the stifle. The severity of the disease varies, but in most cases, it causes the dog considerable pain.

Symptoms, including lameness (especially after exercise) and sometimes obvious swelling of the joints, usually appear when the dog is between four months and one year of age.

Lameness has many possible causes, so x-rays are essential for proper diagnosis.

If the damage to the cartilage is minor, and the osteochondrosis has not progressed to osteochondrosis dissecans, the joint may heal with several weeks of confinement, usually accomplished by crating and leash walking–quite a challenge with a young Lab! More often, though, the damage is severe enough to require surgery. The best prognosis is for pups that have the surgery to prevent severe and potentially crippling arthritis from developing as soon as possible after the disease is diagnosed. Most dogs respond well to surgical treatment for OCD, although results are not quite as promising when the stifle joint is involved. Many dogs live long, sound lives after recovering from OCD surgery, but under no circumstances should a dog that has suffered from OCD be used for breeding.

OCD is thought to be caused by a combination of genetic and environmental factors. OCD of the elbow has been proven to be hereditary in Labrador Retrievers. Whether OCD of other joints is inherited is not yet certain, although there is evidence that dogs whose parents had OCD and dogs that inherit poor structure are more prone to the disease than are others. As with other hereditary problems, the best way to have a healthy puppy is to be sure that the puppy's parents, and preferably its grandparents and older siblings as well, did not suffer from OCD.

Environmental factors can contribute to development of OCD in dogs that have inherited a predisposition for the disease. Poor diet and physical trauma to the joints can cause the cartilage to crack or tear, particularly in dogs that have inherited a tendency for weak cartilage. On the other hand, quality food and moderate exercise can sometimes prevent symptoms of osteochondrosis from developing in the first place, or, if they do, prevent its advancement into OCD.

Patellar Luxation

The patella, or kneecap, is located in the stifle joint in the dog's hind leg. In patellar luxation, the kneecap luxates, or slips out of place, and locks the leg straight. Patellar luxation is not common in Labs, but it does occur and is inherited. Lab puppies should be cleared of patellar luxation either by OFA certification or veterinary examination, and dogs with luxating patellas should not be used for breeding.

Potential Eye Problems in Labs

Inherited eye disease occurs in many breeds (and mixed breed dogs as well). The Labrador Retriever is no exception. Eye problems known to be genetic in Labs include Progressive Retinal Atrophy (PRA), cataracts, and retinal dysplasia.

All Labs used for breeding should have their eyes examined annually by a board certified veterinary ophthalmologist. Some breeders send that evaluation in to the Canine Eye

Registration Foundation (CERF), which in turn issues a CERF certificate good for one year. Many experienced dog fanciers prefer to see a copy of the actual form completed by the ophthalmologist rather than, or in addition to, the CERF certificate. This is because certain conditions may be noted that may be of interest, even though they won't prevent the dog from qualifying for a CERF number.

Progressive Retinal Atrophy

Progressive Retinal Atrophy (PRA) is an inherited condition in which the cells of the retina are destroyed over time. Because the retina absorbs light and enables vision, atrophy of the retina eventually leads to total blindness. Diagnosis of PRA is not easy, and not all veterinary ophthalmologists are able to make the diagnosis. PRA has been a difficult disease to eradicate because symptoms do not appear until the dog is older (commonly 7-8 years old in Labs), by which time it may have been bred.

Two projects are underway to identify the genetic marker for PRA in Labrador Retrievers and other breeds (it has already been identified in Irish Setters). If you have a Lab who appears to be losing his vision, you may be able to help the research effort.

Cataracts

A cataract is an opacity on the lens of the eye that interferes with vision. Not all cataracts are inherited; they can also be caused by injury, other diseases, and old age. Nevertheless, genetically acquired cataracts are a problem in Labrador Retrievers. A dog with a cataract that has no obvious environmental cause should never be used for breeding.

How You Can Help Eradicate PRA in Labs

If your Labrador Retriever is losing his sight, please have him examined for PRA by a veterinary ophthalmologist. If he is diagnosed with PRA (or any genetic eye disease), be sure to let his breeder know. In addition, consider providing samples to further research that may help eradicate PRA in Labs. For more information on submitting samples, contact VetGen at 800-4-VETGEN or fax them at 313-669-8441.

Retinal Dysplasia

Retinal dysplasia is an inherited condition in which the retina develops abnormally. In severe cases, it may interfere with vision, and in some cases, the retina may become detached. Dogs with retinal dysplasia should not be used for breeding.

Eye Clearances

As we've seen, Labs, like many breeds, are prone to some eye problems. If you intend to use your male or female Labrador Retriever for breeding, you should have his or her eyes examined annually by a board certified veterinary ophthalmologist. In addition, you should keep track of you Lab's parents' and sibling's eye clearances at least until the dogs are eight or nine years old. Some diseases, particularly Progressive Retinal Atrophy (PRA), have a late onset, meaning symptoms do not appear until the dog is seven or eight years old.

Even if your dog is altered, you may want to have his eyes examined every few years. If you are participating in sports that require good vision, such as advanced obedience, agility, or fieldwork, you will want to be certain that your dog has no eye disease that will endanger him when jumping or negotiating other obstacles. Even if your Lab is strictly a pet, with no other jobs to do, you might consider having his eyes checked every few years as a part of his on-going health care. If you do, please report the results to your dog's breeder–she needs this information to track the success of her breeding program.

Part Three

Training Your Labrador Retriever

"Marge! The dog's caught his tail again!"

6

Training Your Labrador Retriever

Positive Training Methods

Positive reinforcement, the practice of rewarding desired behavior, gives you a fair and effective way to train your Lab. Please do not take your dog to any training operation that uses punishment and force–modern, knowledgeable obedience instructors encourage training with positive, motivational methods. Some people use "pure" positive reinforcement, meaning that they don't use corrections in training. Rewards in the form of food, toys, and play are used to motivate the dog and reward him for success. Many trainers now use "clickers," small plastic devices used to "mark" correct behavior for the dog with a click, which the dog learns to associate with a reward, usually

Your Labrador Retriever will respond to positive training methods.

Training should begin as soon as you bring your puppy home.

food. Many trainers also use a combination of positive reinforcement for correct behaviors and fair, gentle corrections for unwanted behaviors.

Start training as soon as you bring your puppy home. That roly-poly little Lab baby is quickly going to grow into a big, exuberant dog, and he needs to begin now to learn what you want from him. The main reason that people get rid of young Labrador Retrievers is that the dogs have bad manners and uncontrolled energy and zest for life–and that's nearly always the owner's fault. Your puppy wasn't born knowing what you expect from him. He's a dog. His instincts tell him how to live with dogs. You have to teach him how to live with people. Luckily, thousands of years of domestication have also equipped him with the ability and desire to learn just that. With your guidance, your puppy will happily learn what he needs to know to be the kind of Labrador Retriever everyone dreams of having.

It's important to remember that puppies have little puppy-sized attention spans. Make your training sessions very short, fun, and frequent. Focus on one behavior–"Sit" or "Down" or "Come"–during each session. If your puppy does what you ask two or three times, then quit for a bit and just play with him. You can do a few more minutes of training a little later.

If your Lab is a bit older, the sessions can be a little longer, but even then, frequent, short sessions are more effective than long ones. You want to stop training while your dog still wants to do more, so he'll be thrilled when the next session starts. Don't bore your dog!

Most of us have to work for a living, but in most cases that shouldn't keep us from having canine companionship when we get home. In fairness, though, if you have to be gone all day, be

Training Tip

Be sure all your human family members understand and apply the same "training rules." You need to be consistent to help your puppy learn. If you tell the puppy to stay off the couch but your spouse invites him up, your dog will be confused and you'll be frustrated. (Warning: family members are much harder to train than Labrador Retrievers are!)

Part 3

sure *before* you get the pup that you can make arrangements for his welfare. Puppies are baby mammals, not stuffed toys and not goldfish. It's not fair to ask a puppy to spend eight or nine hours all alone, and it's unreasonable to ask him to wait that long to potty. If you can't come home at lunch time to let him out, play with him, and check on him, consider hiring a pet sitter or other reliable person to come in once or twice during the day to walk him, play with him, and feed him if he still needs a mid-day meal. Your puppy will be happier and healthier, and you won't have quite so much frantic energy to contend with when you do come home. If you can't make proper arrangements for a puppy, then please either postpone getting a pup, or adopt an older dog that can tolerate longer stretches on his own. In that case, please be sure you can spend time with him when you do get home. It's not right to condemn a social creature like a Lab to a life of loneliness.

Chew toys are a great way to keep your dog busy when you don't have time to play.

Give your puppy plenty of toys to play with and chew, but dole them out two or three at a time. If all 37 of his toys are available all the time, your puppy may lose interest. Give him two or three toys at a time–maybe a hard chew toy and a soft puppy toy or rope that he can shake and "kill." Put the rest away. Switch the toys every day or two. If he sees each toy only sometimes, it will be lots more interesting. If his own toys are interesting, it will be a lot easier to teach him what's his and what's not.

Even though you'll do most of your puppy's training at home or when you're out with him, it's still a good idea to take him to a good training class. Your best bet for a young puppy is a puppy kindergarten class with a qualified instructor who can answer your questions, help you get your pup's training off to a good start, and encourage socialization. If your dog is older than six months, look for a basic obedience class.

If you plan eventually to compete in obedience, agility, conformation, or other sports, try to find an instructor who understands your goals. The groundwork for advanced training can be laid very early with good puppy training, and puppies can soak up an amazing

Start teaching the behaviors you want in your adult Lab while he's still a puppy.

amount of information. I taught my Lab, Annie, obedience hand signals before she turned four months old. She never forgot them, even during a long hiatus from training due to elbow problems. If you're serious about training and competing, consider taking more than one class, preferably from different instructors so that you are exposed to different points of view and methods. No dog is fully trained in six or eight weeks, and even if he's doing very well, it's good for your adolescent puppy to continue to have contact with lots of dogs and people.

Beware of any school or trainer who claims to be able to train your dog completely in just a few weeks. Training takes time, and the only short cut is consistency. If the claims seem too good to be true, they are.

Start teaching the behaviors you want in your adult Lab while he's still a puppy. If you don't want your dog to jump on you or lie on the couch when he weighs 70 pounds, don't let him do it as a puppy. It will be a lot easier on both you and your dog if you train for the future right from the start.

How to Approach Dog Training

Wherever you train your dog–at home by yourself, at class, with friends, or with a private instructor–the training process should be fun. That's not to say that things will always go perfectly, of course. Your dog may have trouble learning some things. When that happens, think about how hard it is for you to learn some new things. Now imagine that the new thing you want to learn is being taught to you by an animal that communicates with clucks and whistles. Dogs and people can communicate with one another, but we both have to learn how. Be patient, and if you get frustrated, quit for a while. Come back to the lesson when you're more relaxed.

There are many approaches to dog training. Some of them are a lot alike, while others are very different. Some trainers use food rewards, some don't. Some trainers use choke and pinch collars, some use only flat collars–or no collars at all. Some trainers use clickers (plastic devices that "mark" a correct behavior with a clicking noise for a dog trained in their use), some see clickers as an unnecessary gimmick, and some use clickers part of the time.

Reward your Lab when he does what you ask.

Regardless of what sort of training you decide to pursue with your Lab, there are a few principles that apply. Here are six that are particularly important.

Be consistent. Always use the same command for a behavior, and use that command only for one thing. Your dog has to learn that words have specific meanings. After all, human language is not just a foreign language for him, it's a way of communicating that his own species doesn't use except in response to us. So play fair. For example, "down" should mean one thing and only one thing. If you use it to mean "lie down," then don't also use it to mean "don't jump up" and "get off the couch." (I use "off" to mean "get off" of things").

Be concise. Give a command only once. If you say it three, four, five times, your dog learns to ignore the command.

Be generous. Let your dog know when he's done the right thing by rewarding him. When you teach something new, reward him every single time he does it correctly. A reward can be anything your dog likes–a treat, a ball, a pat, as long as it pleases your dog. Use praise–"nice!" or "pretty!" or whatever you like–with the reward, and your dog will come to enjoy hearing that word as well.

Be smart. If you can't enforce a command, don't give the command unless you're confident that your dog will obey. If you're standing at the back door and it's pouring rain, don't say "come" unless you're willing to go out in the rain, get the dog, and reinforce the command. If you give commands that you can't enforce, your dog will quickly learn that he doesn't

Part 3

have to respond. Your training goal is to teach the dog that he must do what you say when you say it. Mostly we do that for convenience, but control can be a matter of life and death. If you think ahead and are consistent in training, you'll soon have a reliably trained dog.

Always be prepared when getting ready to train your Labrador.

Be prepared. If you need a leash to manage your dog while teaching him to sit, then have the leash on him or nearby before you begin. If your dog doesn't always come when you call him, keep a long line near the back door and put it on him when he goes out to potty so that you can haul him in if necessary. If you are using treats or toys as rewards, have them close at hand so that you can reward your dog immediately for doing well–he won't associate the reward with the behavior unless he's rewarded on the spot.

Be happy. Never forget that your dog is your friend. Labrador Retrievers, for all their joyful goofiness and interest in everything that goes on, really do want to please their people. It's your job to show your Lab what pleases you so he can do it again. Use a happy voice when you give a command and when you praise him. Don't be afraid to get silly–Labs love silly! Put yourself in your dog's place. If someone in authority calls "Come here" in a voice that says "Oh, I'm delighted to see you, please come and stand by me!" and another shouts "Come here" in a tone that says, "You get over here right now," which one would you want to see? Use your voice to tell your dog that you're delighted with him. He'll soon be a lovely, well-trained Lab, and you *will* be delighted!

Six Principles of Training

- Be consistent
- Be concise
- Be generous
- Be smart
- Be prepared
- Be happy

Trying to decide on the "best" way to train your dog can be confusing, and honestly, there is no one best method. Some types of training and equipment work for some dogs but not for others. Some people do well training their dogs one way but not another. In the end, training should be fun for both *you* and your dog, and it should get you the results you want. I use a mishmash of training techniques that I've found work for my dogs and me. Learn about different approaches to dog training, but use whatever works for you and your dog, not someone else. Keep training sessions short so your dog doesn't get bored–remember that Labs just want to have fun! When your dog gets something right, let him know. Make him dance with joy when he sees the training leash in your hand.

Training sessions should be fun for both dog and owner.

Training is the process of helping your puppy to form new habits–habits you want him to have. Your puppy has been learning from the moment he was born–maybe even before that! He's learning all the time, even when you don't think you're teaching him anything. If you allow him to do something you don't like, he learns he can. If you leave him loose in your house unsupervised before he's ready, he learns that he can chew things and potty in the house (unless you've been blessed with a perfect angel of a puppy). It's much easier and faster to prevent bad habits and teach good ones than it is to try to fix bad habits once they're formed.

The Rolled-Up Newspaper Method of Training

If your puppy potties in the house, chews something he shouldn't, or otherwise does something puppyish but not very cute, here's what to do:

- Put your puppy in a safe place
- Get a good sized newspaper
- Roll the paper up and hold it securely in your hand
- Whack yourself in the head three times while repeating, "I will watch the puppy better!"
- Clean up the mess
- Play with your puppy

Never, ever hit your puppy with anything–not your hand, a rolled-up newspaper, or anything else. There's no reason to hit your dog, and it won't teach him anything you want him to learn. Some dogs respond to being hit with fear–they become "hand shy" (afraid of a hand coming toward them) and fearful of people. A frightened dog may become shy, nervous, and withdrawn. Some become so fearful that they bite in self-defense. Other dogs try to fight back. Either way, you will have created an unhappy, potentially dangerous dog–certainly not what you had in mind when you got a Lab for a pet.

Crate Training

Your puppy's crate is your second-best friend. If you use it correctly, the crate will speed up potty training. It will protect your possessions from chewing and other destructive behaviors, and protect your Lab from getting into things that could hurt him. A crate also serves as a safe refuge at home or away. If your dog is properly crate trained, you always have a safe place to put him in an emergency or if he's injured or ill. If you use the crate properly, and never for punishment, your dog will consider it his den. Many dogs love their crates and lie in them even when the doors are open.

Your Lab should feel safe and secure in his crate.

When you're potty training a puppy, his crate should be big enough for him to stand up, turn around, and lie down, but no bigger. Most dogs don't like to sleep where they eliminate, so you don't want to give your puppy room to potty at one end of his crate and go sleep at the other end.

How long can you leave a puppy in a crate? The rule of thumb is that a puppy should be crated for no longer than his age in months plus one. So if your puppy is two months old, don't crate him longer than three hours. If he's six months old, no longer than seven hours. But remember, puppies are all different. If your four-month-old pup does fine in the crate for four hours, but piddles at four and a half hours, then don't leave him longer than four hours without a break. An adult Lab can occasionally tolerate crating for seven or eight hours, but I wouldn't recommend making a practice of that. How would you like to be locked in

Space-Saving Crate Option

A crate is a very important training tool, and when used properly, can become a second home to your dog. However, that second *home* can take up a lot of space in your *home*, which is why the Nylabone® Fold-Away Pet Carrier is so useful. It's a new kind of crate/carrier combo that when not in use, folds easily for storage in a closet or under a bed. When you need it, it can be put together in no time. And it's strong enough for airline travel!

a tiny room with no toilet for eight hours?

Don't put paper or housetraining pads on the bottom of the crate if you're trying to teach your pup not to potty in it. Use a blanket or rug for bedding if your puppy doesn't potty on it or rip it up. If he does, don't give him any bedding.

Your dog's crate should be a good, safe place in his mind. Don't use it to punish him. Feed your puppy in the crate. When you're training him to get into his crate, toss a toy or treat in and say, "Crate!" When he hops in, praise him, close the door, and give him another small treat.

Crate Choices

The crate should be large enough to accommodate your pup as he grows–a "400" size crate, which is about 24" x 36", works for most Labs. In warm weather, your Lab may be more comfortable in a well-ventilated wire crate than in a plastic crate, although if the crate is in your air-conditioned house it won't make much difference. Some wire crates are made to fold up for easy relocation; others are assembled with corner pins. Most plastic crates don't fold, but they are safer for use in a moving vehicle, and are lighter weight than the wire ones. Lightweight PVC and mesh crates are also available, but I don't recommend them for use when you are not present. They're really designed for portability, and are widely used by competitors at obedience and agility trials, but dogs can easily chew their way out of them, and many active dogs roll these crates.

A variety of chew toys in your dog's crate will help keep him occupied.

If Your Lab travels alot, a Nylabone® Fold-Away Pet Carrier is lightweight and easy to assemble.

Check the construction quality. If you purchase a wire crate, be certain the gauge of the wire bars is heavy enough to withstand assaults from strong Labrador teeth and paws. Some puppies, until they become accustomed to the crate, will pull with their teeth or dig with their paws at the wire. A bent wire may be a death trap for a pushy puppy if it can poke its head into the space between the bars.

On a wire crate, a door that overlaps the front wall of the crate is safer than a flush-fitting one, and a secure latch on any crate is vital. I've heard of puppies strangling when they forced their muzzles through as far as their throats and then were unable to pull back out. On plastic crates, the doors are made to lock into the plastic frame, so check that the locking mechanism is secure.

The door latch should be arranged so that the puppy can't reach it and open the crate. Many experienced crate users prefer latches that operate on springs rather than simple sliding latches, or turn-and-lock arrangements that can't be reached from inside the crate.

If you expect to travel with your dog or take him with you in the car a lot, you may find it's worth the extra money to purchase two crates. If you expect to fly your dog, you'll need an airline-approved crate, which is plastic with secure fasteners. For use in a car, or for toting along on a trip, either plastic or wire will work, although in the event of an accident the plastic airline crate will provide better protection for your dog.

You may want to pad the bottom of the crate. Be sure your padding is disposable or washable. Some people use newspaper, but I don't care for its odor, especially after it gets chewed and slobbered a bit. If you use cloth, make it a tightly woven one like an old sheet. Puppies love to pull on threads, and a fuzzy or thready fabric can cause serious problems if the puppy ingests fuzzballs or gets a toenail caught in a loop. Sometimes no blanket or bedding at all is best with a puppy that likes to rip and chew things.

My favorite crate liner for a dog that doesn't chew and rip is a rubber-backed bathroom rug. These rugs don't slip or slide much on the crate bottom, they're comfy for puppy naps, and best of all, they wash up beautifully. Just don't use chlorine bleach or you'll have rubber backing all over the bottom of your dryer!

Housetraining

Housetraining is, to most people, the most immediate and important training a puppy needs. If you are diligent about getting the puppy out to potty when he needs to go, and patient when he does have an accident, housetraining your Labrador Retriever should go quickly and smoothly.

Keep in mind that a puppy doesn't have complete control and may have a few accidents. My Lab, Raja, used to leave a little trail of urine as he ran to the door–he was trying his best but just couldn't quite turn off the tap. Most puppies can't control their bowels completely until they're a few months old, and not fully until they are adults. It's up to you to anticipate his needs and be prepared for a few accidents. Expect your pup to need to urinate and defecate shortly after he wakes up, after he has eaten, and after he has been playing a while. If you take him out to his "place" immediately after he wakes up or eats, he'll learn very quickly to go outside to potty.

Bring Your Lab puppy to the same spot to eliminate.

When he's playing in the house, keep a close eye on him, and if he starts to sniff around, turn in circles, or arch his back slightly while walking, *pick him up and take him out.* If you want him to learn to use a particular part of the yard, take him there on leash and stay with him until he finishes. Soon he'll form the habit of going there and nowhere else, especially if you keep the area clear of feces. Remember, once a baby starts to go potty, he can't stop if he's on his own feet, so help him get to the right place. As he gets older and has more control, he'll be able to race out the door when you open it and do his business where you want it. When he does relieve himself in the right place, praise him with a happy voice and petting.

Establishing Household Rules

As with all other training, consistency is the key when teaching your puppy the rules of the household. First, be sure all your human family members understand the rules so that everyone uses the same ones!

Decide about the basics before you bring your puppy home. It's very confusing for a young pup to be allowed certain privileges when he's a pudgy 10 weeks of age and then suddenly have them removed when he's a lanky 16 weeks old. If you don't want your adult Lab on the couch or bed, don't let him be there as a baby.

Training in good basic manners should also start immediately. *The single most loving thing you can do for your puppy is to train him.*

A word of caution. Puppies do have accidents, and adults who haven't been taught where to go may have a few as well. Never punish a dog for an accident–don't rub his nose in it, or hit him, or yell. Help him to make the right decisions, and reward him for success. If your puppy isn't reliable in the house, don't leave him unsupervised. If he does have an accident, take him outside. Clean the spot with a good odor and stain remover (available at pet supply stores) so that it isn't "labeled" as a potty place. Most dogs prefer to keep their homes–their dens–clean, but they need some guidance to learn how.

Training Basics

Despite the image our popular culture gives us, your puppy didn't arrive in the world knowing what you want him to do, and you didn't arrive knowing how to train your dog. Granted, lots of people and dogs muddle along, spending years loving one another but not quite understanding one another. Too many Americans seem to think that poor behavior is just part of being a dog and that putting up with poor behavior is part of loving a dog. Not so! Your dog will be much happier if you learn to train him properly, and you'll be much happier if he's trained and mannerly. Who wants to live with a brat–especially a 70-pound energetic Labrador brat?

But won't you break your dog's spirit by training him? No. Not if you use positive motivational training methods and approach training with patience, a sense of humor, and willingness to learn from your dog and from knowledgeable trainers and instructors. You'll have control of your dog without shouting and getting frustrated, and your dog will be a secure, well-behaved companion who will trust that you know what you're doing. The bond of trust and understanding that comes from training can only enhance your relationship with your dog–not to mention with your family members and friends who spend time with your dog.

If your Lab learns that training sessions are fun, he'll learn quickly. Your goal from the start should be to built trust, mutual respect, and understanding between yourself and your puppy. The bond you build when he's young will see you both through your dog's adolescence (something like the "terrible twos" in children) and beyond.

Begin training when your Lab is a puppy and reinforce the training as he gets older.

Obedience training is simply the process of teaching your dog to do what you tell him to do. For some dogs that means learning complex commands for competitive and non-competitive sports, police and detection work, service work for disabled owners, and other demanding forms of work. For most dogs, obedience training means learning basic manners, a few commands, and maybe some fun tricks.

Obedience training is simply the process of teaching your dog to do what you tell him to do.

There's lots of information available in books and magazines and on the Internet about effective, humane methods of dog training, and there are good obedience instructors in most areas of the country. The information that follows in this chapter will get you started, but please don't stop here. Continue learning and training–I think you'll find you enjoy your dog a lot more.

Training Tools

As with any activity, using the right equipment will make your training efforts more effective. The hard part is deciding what's right. Ask three dog trainers or obedience instructors what kind of collar or leash is "best" for training a Labrador Retriever and you'll probably get three opinions. Here's the answer: the best piece of equipment for your dog is the one that works best for you and the dog at a particular time for a

A collar and leash are useful tools when training Your Labrador Retriever.

particular purpose. You may need one type of collar when your Lab is a silly adolescent and another when he matures and acts more sensible. You may prefer a short leash for teaching your dog to walk politely or heel and a longer one for other exercises. You may even want to experiment–what works well for someone else or one dog may not work for you or for this dog. I vary the collars I use depending on the individual dog's age, level of training, personality, and the type of training. Several types of collars are commonly used for basic and more advanced training. Let's look at some basic training equipment.

Collars

A flat collar is a leather, nylon, or fabric collar fastened with a buckle or a quick-release clasp. This is the collar that should carry your dog's name, license, and rabies tags and is the only type of collar that should stay on your dog when you are not actively training him. A flat collar should fit so that you can slide two fingers between the collar and your dog's neck. If it's too loose, your dog may be able to slip out of it or may easily get it caught on something. A flat collar is the only collar that should be used on a young puppy, as other types of collars can easily injure a delicate young neck. Flat collars are often the only kind allowed in "clicker" or positive motivation only classes. The problem with a flat collar is that it doesn't give you much control, and with a strong young Lab that can be a serious problem.

Beware of Dog

Don't leave a puppy alone with a collar on. It could get entangled in something, and the puppy could accidentally choke himself.

A martingale collar looks like a flat collar but has no buckle. It slips on over your dog's head. When you pull against it with your leash, a properly fitted martingale tightens enough to keep your dog from slipping out of the collar but not enough to choke the dog. This collar gives a bit more control than a flat collar. Martingales are used in agility, flyball, and some other dog sports, as well as with dogs that have a tendency to duck and pull their way out of a flat collar.

Toys can be used as rewards when training.

The choke chain (also called a slip chain, slip collar, or training collar) is usually made of metal chain, although they also come in nylon and leather. Many good dog trainers use choke chains without being cruel to their dogs, but it is very easy to misuse a choke chain, and most people do. Many people use collars that don't fit the dog or put the choke collars on incorrectly. Either way, the collars are ineffective, and many dogs learn to ignore them. Worse yet, choke chains can permanently injure your dog's throat.

Choke chains were traditionally used for a style of dog training referred to as "pop and jerk" because the method relied on jerking the leash to tighten the collar quickly, causing the dog pain, which the dog sought to avoid. Knowledgeable dog trainers and obedience instructors no longer use "pop and jerk" training methods, which are based on fear and punishment, although some still use choke chains in some circumstances.

A choke chain must be put on correctly to work properly. First, it must fit correctly. I often see dogs wearing choke chains that are two or three times longer than they should be for the size of the dog. A choke chain should fit your dog so that when you pull the moveable end of the chain (the "live ring") through the "dead ring" (the one that the chain slides through), two to three inches of chain remain. If your dog has a very large head, you may have to allow a little more chain for putting on and taking off the collar, but never more than a few inches. Next, the collar needs to be on the right way around. When you stand with your dog on your left, both of you facing the same direction, the live ring moves the chain through the dead ring across the top of the dog's neck. If the live ring crosses under the dog's neck, the collar is on backwards.

Finally, a choke chain needs to be used properly. If you don't know how to use one, please take your dog to an obedience class to learn how (assuming you decide to use a choke chain at all). The idea of the collar is not to keep a strangle hold on your dog but to correct him when he makes a mistake. Yet how many times have you seen a dog pulling his owner

Your Lab's collar should have his ID tags so that he can be identified if lost.

along, gagging and coughing but paying little attention to his choke chain?

The halter (also known as a head collar) looks something like a horse halter. It controls the dog's head on the principle that where the head goes, the body follows. Many Lab owners use halters, which they find more effective than many other collars because Labs have strong necks and high pain thresholds. In fact, halters are so effective that some people never actually train their dogs and end up with dogs that are controllable with their halters on, but not with them off. So if you decide to use a halter to get control of your neck-strong Lab, please also teach your dog to obey obedience commands.

The prong collar (also called a pinch collar) may look like a medieval torture device, and many people are opposed to prong collars. However, used properly the prong collar is an effective training tool for large, strong dogs and for many dogs that become overexcited. You really can't do much training if you can't control the dog or get his attention. A prong collar gives control when nothing else does–I've used small prong collars effectively on my rowdy young Labs without causing them any apparent discomfort.

The prong collar applies pressure from the prongs to points around the dog's neck. You can adjust the collar so that it uses no prongs, a few, or all the prongs. Prong collars give better control with less force, and studies have shown that prong collars are less likely to injure a dog's neck and throat than are choke chains. As with a choke chain, though, it's important to have the collar fitted properly, so have a knowledgeable obedience instructor (not a salesperson in a pet supply store) show you how to fit the collar and how to use it properly.

Some people see electronic collars (shock collars) as a quick and easy way to train a dog. Unfortunately, most people who use shock collars use them incorrectly to punish the dog for doing something wrong rather than to teach him what he should do. A shock collar can cause more problems than you had to begin with. I do not recommend shock collars for most dog owners or dogs. You and your dog will be much better off spending that money on a good obedience class.

A Good Leash (or Two)

A collar won't do you much good without a leash. In fact, I suggest you get two leashes, in case one gets lost or chewed. *Don't* buy a chain leash. It's ineffective for training, hard on your hands, and if it swings with any force at all it can injure your dog or you. I don't care for nylon leashes, either. They chafe and can cut your hands and legs if a whirling Labrador wraps one around you. Leather leashes, the first choice of experienced trainers, are strong, easier on your hands, and effective training tools. Leather leashes come in various widths and strengths. Choose one that is three-fourths to one inch wide and that has a securely fastened slide bolt for attaching it to your dog's collar. Check out the construction quality. The hand loop and buckle should be stitched securely. If the leather is stiff, you can soften it up by cleaning it regularly with saddle soap, which is available from most shoe or tack stores.

Leashes come in several lengths. Many dog trainers like six-foot leashes but I'm uncoordinated enough to find that much length hard to manage except for specialized training. I prefer a three- to four-foot leash for most training. For walking, the best leash is one that allows some slack but not so much that the dog gets tangled up all the time, or a retractable leash if you prefer.

Since you'll be handling a big dog with your leash, here's a safety tip: never slip the loop on a leash over your wrist or any other part of your body. A sudden lunge of an excited Lab could break your wrist or pull you over. Teach your children this rule, too, and enforce it. An excited Lab can easily drag a child or pull her into traffic. Safety first!

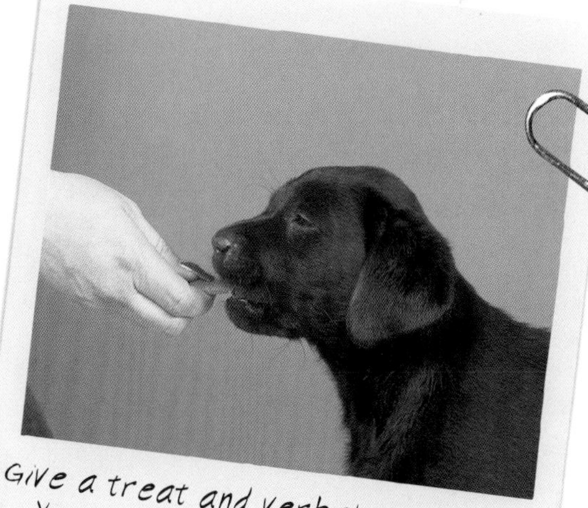

Give a treat and verbal praise when your Lab does something right.

Rewards

I suggest that you use treats for training rewards. Most Labrador Retrievers are very motivated by food. (If your dog truly isn't interested in food, then find a toy or a certain ear scratch or something that does tickle him.) Remember, you're not using training treats to feed you dog, but rather to reward him for a job well done. Once your dog has learned the command and does it reliably, you don't need to reward with food. You should still reward him with praise most of the time, though, and a treat once in a while for a job well done certainly won't hurt.

Use small, tasty bits of foods that are soft and easily chewed. You want your dog to gobble the treat and focus again on training, not stop to chew. Treats are more interesting if your dog doesn't know what may be coming next, so try putting together a "training trail mix" of things your dog likes. Some good, interesting treats include plain unsweetened cereal, string cheese, plain air-popped popcorn, thinly sliced hot dogs (you can microwave the slices to reduce greasiness–three to five minutes usually works), tiny or soft dog treats, a little dry cat food, tiny bits of apple–whatever your dog thinks is yummy. My dog, Rowdy, will do anything for a bit of carrot! Many trainers use a small pouch on a belt to hold their training treats to avoid messy pockets–a small fanny pack works well.

The Right Words at the Right Times

You also need two special words for training. First, you need a praise word. This is a word you use to tell your dog he's done something right. At first, say the word as you give your dog a treat. He'll quickly learn that the word is a good thing. Try to find a word that you don't use all the time with your dog. If you're like me, you tell your dog he's a "good boy" even when he hasn't done anything except be your wonderful dog, so "good boy" won't be effective as a reward. I use "pretty!" or "very nice" to praise my dogs in training.

A trained dog is a happier dog.

You also need a release word to tell your dog when he's finished working on something. For instance, when you tell your dog to "sit," he should sit and remain sitting until you tell him he doesn't have to anymore. You need a word to tell him that. Many people use "OK" for a release word, which is fine if it works for you. But many of us say "OK" a lot in our general speech, and you don't want to release your dog by accident. I use "free!" for my release word. The word itself doesn't matter, but it should be one you can remember, and that you don't use frequently.

Teaching your Lab the basic commands early will ensure that he grows to be a well-mannered adult.

Basic Obedience Commands

Do you enjoy standing at your back door calling a dog that ignores you? Do you like to lock your dog up when company comes because he won't lie down and stay put when you tell him? We all know dogs like that–most of us have lived with them. The sad fact is that people teach their own dogs to ignore them! Any reasonably healthy dog of any breed can be trained to respond to basic commands, and every dog deserves to be taught good manners. You can start teaching the basics as soon as your puppy comes home. A mannerly dog is a pleasure to live with and to introduce to your friends. A rude dog is neither. And the unbridled enthusiasm of an untrained Labrador Retriever will make him a nuisance and possibly a menace.

Come, sit, down, stay, and leave it–five simple commands can make all the difference in your relationship to your dog. I'll tell you how to teach your dog to respond to each of the five basic commands. This will get you started, but you should still take your Lab through at least a basic obedience class. If possible, start your puppy with a puppy kindergarten class for socialization and feedback from the instructor.

Come

A dog that comes reliably when called is safer than one that doesn't, and the owner of a dog that comes when called is usually a lot happier than the owner of a dog that blows him off. Here's my way of training a dog to come reliably.

Begin with your puppy or dog on leash or in a small fenced area or room where he can't get too far away. Have a treat or toy ready. You can use any word you like for calling your dog–"come," "here," "by me," whatever, as long as you use it consistently. Precede the command with your dog's name to get his attention. So, for instance, your command may

You need your Lab's undivided attention during training sessions.

be, "Rover, come!" Always use a playful, happy voice when you call your dog, and use the command only once. Then do whatever you have to do to get your dog to come to you. Do not walk toward the dog. If he's avoiding the command, his natural response will be to move away from you as you approach. Instead, turn away, walk or run the other way, crouch down, act goofy, play with the toy–anything to make him curious enough to come to you. Reward him the instant he gets to you. Use your praise word and play with him, give him a treat, or give him a toy. Then let him go back to what he was doing. Repeat the process two or three times before quitting for this session. Do this several times a day if possible.

If your dog doesn't come when you call despite your best efforts, gently guide him toward you with the leash. When he starts to move toward you on his own, let the leash go slack, but encourage him with happy talk and by moving away to speed him up, and reward him when he gets to you.

Training Rules

There are some things that you should always do when training your dog as well as a few things to never do. Follow these rules and training will be a snap.

- *Always* use the same word when giving a command.
- *Never* give a command more than once—if you do, you'll teach your dog to ignore you.
- *Always* reward your dog for obeying your command—the reward may be a treat, a little play, praise, a toy, as long as you acknowledge that he's done well. Nobody likes to be ignored after doing a good job!
- *Never* let your dog off leash in an unfenced area if you don't have 100 percent confidence that he will follow your commands.
- *Never* give your dog a command if you can't enforce it. If you keep giving a command and he doesn't respond, you're just teaching him that he doesn't have to obey.

If you're training in a small space with no leash, put the leash on him for a while. Keep the leash on until he's responding reliably, then try again with it off. If he regresses, go back to the leash for a while. If you're persistent, he will learn.

Your goal should be to make yourself the most attractive, interesting thing in your dog's world. Never call your dog to you to lock him up or do something he doesn't like–go get him instead.

During a play session, call your dog to you several times, reward, and then let him go back to playing. Don't teach him that coming when you call means the end of the fun. Always reward him for coming with praise, petting, play, a toy, or a treat. Occasionally give him a "jackpot"–a combination of several treats, petting, his favorite toy, and play.

If you want your dog to respond when other people call him, you can make a game of calling the dog back and forth with other family members or friends. Use the same training principles as you use alone. Make sure that only one person calls at a time, and each person rewards the dog for responding. Most Labs think this is a great game.

Teaching your Lab to sit is fairly easy. The sit command is useful in many situations.

Sit

Stop a moment and consider that nearly everyone who has a pet dog manages to teach that dog to sit on command. So how come so many dogs are untrained? Remember, if you can teach your Lab to sit on command, you can teach him anything!

"Sit" is a useful command. It can be used to control a rowdy dog. "Sit" gives you control over your dog on walks (teaching sit at the curb before crossing the street makes you both safer), at the vet, and at home. So let's teach "sit."

Start with your dog on leash or confined in a small area. Hold a small treat in front of his nose, but don't let him take it. When he shows interest in the treat, *slowly* raise the treat and move it back over his head toward his tail. As his head comes up to follow the treat, his butt has to go down. When he starts to fold his hind legs into the sit, tell him, "Sit." Keep moving the treat slowly backward. The instant he sits completely, give him the treat and praise him. Then release him with your release word. Be sure to give him the treat *before* you release him and only if he is sitting. If he gets up, repeat the procedure until he sits, then reward him quickly while he's sitting. If you give him the treat when he's not sitting, you're rewarding him for not sitting. Work for three or four successful repetitions at a time and then quit. If you do several sessions a day, your dog should sit on command in no time. When he sits promptly on command, lengthen the time he has to remain sitting before you give him the treat. Start with a few seconds, gradually increasing to half a minute, then a minute. Your dog should stay sitting until you release him or give him another command.

Down

There are many ways to teach a dog to down (lie down). I like to teach "down" from a stand rather than a sit for three reasons. First, "down" can save your dog's life, and is a safer command than "come" at times. Suppose your dog gets away from you and crosses the street. A car is coming. You don't want to call your dog, because he might be hit. You don't want to ignore him, because he may wander further away or decide to come back across the street at the wrong moment. If he will lie down on command, you can keep him safe.

Teaching the down command can be challenging, but it can save your dog's life.

On a less dramatic level, teaching "down" from a sit requires two commands–"sit" and then "down." I'm lazy, and I'd rather just give one command most of the time. Finally, if you are training for advanced obedience competition, you'll have to teach your dog a "drop" in which he lies down from a trot on the recall. If your dog sits first and then lies down, he'll creep forward a little and have a slow drop. If he just drops, he won't. Here's how I teach "down."

Start with your dog standing. Kneel beside him at first if that's easier for you. Hold a treat in your hand, and let your dog know it's there. Slowly move your hand toward and then between your dog's front legs, lowering it as you go. He should lie down as his nose follows the treat. If he lowers only his front end, gently guide his rear down. The instant he's completely down, praise him and give him the treat. If he steps backwards instead of lying down, move the treat toward him and down a little faster–that will get his head and neck down faster and he should go down.

Don't force your dog to sit if he doesn't want to.

If his butt stays up in the air once his front end is down, and he doesn't lower it with a gentle touch of your hand, don't try to force him. Keep the treat close to the ground and cradle your dog's hind legs from behind with your other arm. Move your arm forward gently until he folds his legs and lies down. When he's all the way down, praise him and give him the treat. Then release him. Pretty soon he'll be dropping into a down on command. Slowly increase the amount of time he has to stay down before getting the treat.

Stay

"Stay" is a very important command. You can use it to tell your dog not to move, whether he's standing on an examining table at the veterinarian's, sitting in your car, or lying on his bed in the family room.

Many people teach "stay" first with the sit. I prefer to teach "stay" initially in the down position because it's easiest for a dog to hold a down. If he learns the concept of "stay" in the down, he can transfer it more easily to other, more challenging positions. Let's teach "stay."

Once your dog has learned to lie down on command, begin to teach him "stay" as an extension of the down. Begin with your dog on leash. When he is completely down, praise and reward him, then tell him, "Stay." If he starts to get up, put him back in the down

Teaching a Lab pup to stay takes patience.

position, praise him, but don't give him a treat. Tell him, "Stay," again. If he stays down a few seconds, praise, reward, and release.

Start with very short stays of less than a minute and stay very close to your dog. Gradually increase the length of the stay until your dog will stay about five minutes with you standing close to him. When he will stay for five minutes, put him in the down-stay, and take one step away from him. Have him stay for 30 seconds, then step back to him, praise, reward, and release. Build the time up again gradually to five minutes. Repeat this process to gain distance and time. Whenever you increase your distance away from your dog, reduce the amount of time you require him to stay, and then increase the time again gradually. If he gets up before the time is up, reduce the distance until he's solid again at that distance and time. Then increase the distance by one or two steps, and shorten the time. This approach may seem tedious, but trust me–if you work through this approach patiently and systematically, in a month or two your dog should have a good stay when you are some distance from him. That beats unreliable stays–or none at all–for the life of your dog! Remember, too, that you must always be the one who ends the stay by releasing your dog. Don't let him decide that he's done. If he can release himself after ten minutes, why not after one?

When your dog is doing a reasonably solid down stay for three minutes with you six feet away, repeat the same process with him in a sit. Stay very close at first and keep the time very short. Slowly increase the time, then increase the distance and shorten the time, then slowly build up the time again, and so on. You can teach the stand-stay following the same procedure.

When your dog stays reliably, start practicing stays while you're doing other things. Just don't get so distracted that you forget and let him wander away. If you want your Lab to follow commands reliably, teach him that you are reliable and consistent, too.

Leave It!

"Leave it" is a very handy command. With it you can tell your dog not to smooch with the pretty Sheltie at obedience class, not to swipe the cookie you set on the coffee table while you get your book to read, and not to touch that disgusting pile of whatever-it-is on the sidewalk.

When you teach "leave it," you need to reward the dog for leaving whatever he's after, and the reward has to be worthwhile in his eyes (or mouth!). Make sure that you have control of the situation and can effectively keep your dog from getting "it," because if he gets whatever he's after, he's been rewarded for ignoring your command to "leave it."

To begin, put something that you know will interest your dog on the floor or a low table. It should not be something he normally plays with–that's not fair. It could be a bit of food, a toy, or anything else he's likely to try to pick up. Have some wonderful treats ready. Put your dog on leash. Walk your dog near the temptation–and be sure the leash is short enough that you can keep him from getting it. As soon as he shows interest in the object, tell him, "Leave it!" and walk quickly away–he'll have to follow you because of the leash. You could just give a quick tug on the leash and reward him when he looks at you, but when first teaching "leave it" I like to keep moving so the dog refocuses quickly. As soon as your dog looks at you instead of the temptation, praise and reward him. Make a big fuss about what a good dog he is. You want him to know that you're better than anything, anywhere. Repeat the process three or four times per session. After a few sessions, your dog should be responding nicely to "leave it," and you can start using it on walks and in other settings. Remember to reward him for complying! Eventually you won't need to reward your dog with treats for leaving things, but always praise him for obeying this command. You know how hard it is to resist temptation!

A couple of warnings about teaching this command. First, if your dog manages to get the object of his desire before you get him away from it, you need to take it from him if possible. If it's a toy, take it from him, put it back where it was, and repeat the training routine and make sure he doesn't get it this time! If you're using food, you take it from him if possible. *Caution–do not* try to take food away if your dog growls or has a tendency to guard food–in fact, if that's the case, don't use food for teaching "leave it." You could get bitten. Get some help to get the guarding behavior under control. Do not under any circumstances allow a child to teach the leave it command.

Puppy kindergarten classes allow your dog to socialize with other dogs his age and learn in the process.

Types of Training Classes

Whatever kind of training you want to try with your Labrador Retriever, there's probably a class for you somewhere. Here are some of the more common types of dog-training classes offered in many areas.

Puppy Kindergarten Classes

Puppy kindergarten classes are usually for puppies from about two to five months old. A good puppy kindergarten class gives your puppy a chance to interact with other puppies for socialization. All play should be supervised closely, especially if there's a wide range of size and age among the puppies. The puppies should also interact with the other puppies' owners during classes. Most classes also teach the puppies to sit, lie down, and come on command and to walk politely on leash. Good puppy kindergarten classes also cover potty training, socialization, developmental periods, problem behaviors, grooming, and other topics of interest.

Puppy kindergarten classes usually meet once a week for five to eight weeks. A class has advantages over training alone at home. First, you make a commitment to train at a specific time. You will also have daily homework exercises, and in doggy school, everyone knows who did and didn't do their homework. Second, going to class is another opportunity for your puppy to be socialized with other people and with all sorts of dogs. You'll also learn a lot from watching your classmates and their pups, and you'll have your instructor to help you if you have a training problem.

Going to School

Training at home is necessary and good, but a good training class will give you a chance to train you Lab to behave and to obey you even when there are lots of distractions. A class also gives you feedback—the instructor can help when something isn't working and can tell you when you're doing something that inadvertently undermines your dog's training.

If you plan to compete eventually, you may be able to find a puppy "competition" obedience or agility class. Young Labs shouldn't jump or participate in other repetitive activities that put stress on their bones and joints until their bones mature, but they can start on low obstacles and learn to follow directions.

Basic Obedience Classes

Basic obedience classes are normally for dogs five months old or older. A good basic obedience class will, more than anything, teach you how to train your dog. Most basic classes focus on, well, the basics: sit, down, stay, come, and walking politely on leash.

Competition Obedience Classes

Competition obedience classes teach you how to train your dog to compete in obedience trials. They focus on your handling skills as well as techniques for teaching the dog the advanced exercises.

Conformation Classes

Conformation classes prepare dogs to show in conformation, which is what many people think of when we say "dog show." Some classes provide training for the handler, but many simply provide practice time for the dog. If you want to learn how to show your dog, look for a handling class, which will teach you how to show your dog in conformation dog shows.

Agility Classes

Agility classes teach you to train your dog to compete in agility. Your dog should be finished growing before you enroll him in a regular agility course, but some training schools offer puppy agility classes designed to teach basics without stressing immature bones and joints.

Whatever your training goal, always remember your dog's your friend.

Therapy Dog Training

Therapy dog training prepares you and your dog to visit nursing homes, hospitals, schools, and other facilities, bringing the residents love, joy, and "warm fuzzies."

Field Training Classes

Field training classes and private lessons are available from many Labrador Retriever and other sporting clubs as well as private trainers. Field training prepares you and your dog for hunt tests and field trials.

Choosing a Class

The quality of training offered by clubs and private schools varies widely. Here are some things to ask as you investigate places to train your dog.

- How big is the class? If there are more than ten people and dogs, will the instructor have a qualified assistant? Will you get individual help when you need it?
- Are the facilities adequate and reasonably clean? Is there room for class members to move about safely, without being jammed together? Is the footing good so you and your dog won't slip? Is the outdoor potty area kept reasonably clean?
- Are health policies in place? Are all dogs required to show proof of vaccination for common infectious diseases? If you prefer not to vaccinate annually, are titres acceptable? Are dogs expected to be reasonably clean and free of fleas?
- Are there policies to keep you and your dog safe? What if a dog in your class displays aggression toward other dogs or people?

A new chew toy is a great reward for following commands properly.

Training at Home

Most of your training will be done away from your training classes. You need to work on what you learn in class with daily practice at home. Several short sessions–10 to 20 minutes–during the day are more effective than one long one. Labs are intelligent dogs, and long repetitious sessions will bore the both of you. Keep it fun!

Take advantage of training opportunities whenever they present themselves. If you're teaching your dog a new command, have him do it for his dinner, to get his leash on for a walk, at the door when he wants out, and so on. Practice stays while you watch TV or polish the silver. Practicing commands in different situations will help your dog learn that the command means the same thing whether she's in the kitchen or at doggy school or out in the back yard.

Is This the Right Obedience Instructor for my Dog and Me?

Here are some questions to ask about the training instructor. The answer should be yes to most of them. If you don't feel comfortable about the instructor's knowledge, attitude, or methods, go somewhere else. Never let an instructor handle your dog unless you are completely confident that she won't do something you don't want her to do.

√ Does the instructor have a history of success training dogs and teaching classes? Lengthy experience doesn't always provide knowledge or good teaching skills, but if your instructor is teaching a class for the first time, she should have successful training experience with her own dogs, and experience assisting another instructor.

√ Does the instructor have some educational background about dogs and dog training? Has she attended seminars, workshops, or advanced classes? Has she kept up current knowledge about how dogs (and people) learn? Don't be shy about asking what her credentials are.

√ Does the instructor belong to the National Association of Dog Obedience Instructors (NADOI), the Association of Pet Dog Trainers (APDT), or another professional organization?

√ Does the instructor communicate well with people? Does she listen carefully and respond clearly? Do dogs respond to her positively? Are her own dogs reasonably well trained?

√ Does the instructor appear to really like dogs? Does she appear to like people and enjoy teaching? Does she praise her students and encourage them to praise their dogs?

√ Is the instructor flexible and creative in her approach to dogs that have problems? A good dog trainer adapts to the needs of the individual dog, and a good instructor will help you find a method that works with your dog.

7

Solving Problem Behavior

Nobody's perfect, not even your beautiful Labrador Retriever. But if you plan ahead and respond promptly, you can prevent most problem behaviors before they begin, and you can fix most others with reasonable ease. Most canine behaviors are either instinctive or learned. (A few may be caused by medical or environmental problems.) The best way to deal with a behavior problem is to use what we know about canine behavior and instincts to prevent undesirable behaviors before they occur. The next best approach is to keep the dog from repeating an unwanted behavior and to replace it with one that's acceptable. Remember back in Chapter 2 when I talked about breeds being developed for specific purposes? If you know

Preventing problem behaviors takes time and effort.

The best way to control undesirable behaviors is to prevent them before they occur.

what your Lab's genes are telling him to do, you understand his behavior better, and you'll be able to find a behavior that satisfies your dog's instincts without disturbing your human sensibilities.

The most important thing you can do to prevent problem behaviors is to stay in control. If your puppy likes to chew and rip things up, then don't leave him loose when you're gone or can't supervise him. That's what your crate is for! If your dog digs holes when he's alone in the yard for 20 minutes, don't leave him alone in the yard for more than 15 minutes–or give him a place to dig. If your Lab loves to run when he has the chance and won't come back when you call, don't let him off leash in an unfenced area.

Lack of exercise is a major cause of behavior problems in Labs, especially young Labs. Again, look to the breed's original purpose. Your Lab was designed over many generations to have the energy to retrieve fowl for hunters all day long. A young Lab needs to run–and run and run and run. A tired dog is a good dog, but one with pent-up energy is going to look for ways to spend it. He just has to! So be sure your dog gets plenty of exercise. Sending him out alone to the backyard for an hour doesn't count. He needs someone to play ball with him, take him for a long walk, or *something* every single day.

Your Lab's mind needs to work, too. Boredom often leads to behavioral problems. Find things for your Lab to think about. Some toys are designed to provide mental stimulation–for example, there are a number of toys on the market that randomly dispense bits of food as the dog manipulates them. Caution, though–don't leave such a toy with your Lab when you're not there–he may decide to stop fooling with the "puzzle" and just bite the darn thing open, and a broken toy can be dangerous.

Training will also relieve boredom and the behavior problems it causes. Teach your dog silly tricks or train him for competitive obedience, agility, fieldwork, or tracking–it doesn't matter what, as long as it involves mental and physical exercise. Training, particularly obedience training, will quite simply make your Lab a better canine companion across the board. Even when you don't work on a specific behavior problem in training, a dog that learns to behave and obey in one setting usually behaves better in other settings. That's partly because the dog expends physical and mental energy in training, but it's also because an obedience-trained dog knows what you want and trusts you.

Some Common Problems

When your puppy or dog does something you don't like, you need to teach him not to do it. Here are three general ideas that should help you deal with most problems.

First, figure out why your dog is doing what he's doing. Trust me–he's not doing it to get back at you for something. Dogs just don't do that. So look for a real canine motivation, not an imagined human one. Is he following some deep instinct bred into ancestors for many generations? Is he full of energy and lacking enough exercise? Is he using this behavior to get something he wants?

Next, be sure that you're the one in control. I had a Lab years ago that trained me to go get him a treat. He'd come and bark at me, I'd get up and follow him, he'd point to the biscuits, bark again, and I'd tell him how clever he was and give him a cookie. Then one day I realized that he had me trained! Well, the rules quickly changed. When he barked at me, I gave him a command, turning the tables on him. Sometimes that was it–he forgot about the biscuit. Sometimes he got a belly rub or a game of fetch or catch. Other times, I'd have a wonderful idea–let's get a cookie! Off we'd go to the biscuits, and after he obeyed another couple of commands, he got a biscuit. I was back in control, and he was quite content. If your Lab is a bit pushy, as mine was–and many are, especially about food!–make him earn whatever you give him. Expand his repertoire–teach him some tricks. Your dog will be a lot happier if he knows for sure you're the one in charge.

Training and exercise will help your Lab be well-behaved.

Next, whenever possible teach your dog an acceptable behavior as an alternative to the one you don't like. Some ideas are discussed in the following pages, but I can't cover every possibility here, so remember this: *it's a lot easier to teach your dog to do something than to teach him to do nothing.*

Finally, if you run into a behavior problem that endangers people, your dog, or other animals, or one that you can't fix in a reasonable amount of time, find a qualified dog trainer or behaviorist who can help. Don't let a small problem become a big one. Now let's see how you can solve some common behavior problems.

Jumping On People

Your Labrador Retriever doesn't jump on you to see what your shirt will look like with muddy paw prints, to annoy you, or to get even with you for taking away that yummy tennis shoe. He jumps up because he likes you. He jumps also because, if you're like most people, you unwittingly reward him for the behavior by getting excited (what fun!), petting him, pushing him (which he sees as play), and paying attention to him. He thinks you're enjoying his game.

Jumping up to get a drink is one thing, but jumping up on people is another.

If you want your dog to stop jumping up, you have to learn to be consistent in your response, and not to reward him. Don't push him down with your hands and then pet him–if you do, you're telling him he's done well. Don't try to catch him in the chest with your knee–you probably won't connect, and if you do may injure your dog. Even rough-and-tumble Labrador Retrievers get hurt. If your dog wasn't trained not to jump up while he was a puppy, then try one of the following approaches.

One technique that works with some dogs is to completely ignore him when he's jumping. Wear old clothes for this! When your dog jumps up on you, don't give him any attention. Cross your arms over your chest, turn your back on the dog, and look at the sky. He'll probably keep trying for a little while, especially if he's used to getting a livelier response out of you. Sooner or later, though, he'll realize that you become boring when he jumps on you, and he'll quit. When he stops jumping, pet him and talk to him quietly. Don't get him all excited, but tell him he's a good dog. If he starts to jump up again (which he may do the first few times) become boring again. You need to be patient to make this method work, but it does work. Just don't sabotage your hard work by getting near your dog with clothes you really don't want him to jump on. Plan ahead until he's reliable.

If your dog has had obedience training and knows some other commands, try using a positive command like "sit" or "down" before he jumps. If he responds correctly, reward him. There are two problems with this approach. Obviously, he has to know the command you use, so puppies and dogs that don't have much training don't respond well. The other problem is that your dog may think the reaction he gets when he jumps up is more rewarding than the reward he gets for sitting or lying down. If so, try the "boring" approach described above.

Destructive Chewing

Chewing is a terrifically pleasurable activity for many dogs. A nice raw bone (no cooked bones, please; they can splinter) or Nylabone® is oh so satisfying. Unfortunately, if your dog doesn't limit his chewing to legal chewies, he can cause a lot of damage to property and to himself.

Destructive chewing can be redirected by providing a variety of chew toys for your Lab.

The best cure for problem chewing is prevention. If your Lab likes to chew and rip things up, then don't leave him loose with unsupervised access to things you don't want him to chew–ever. This is one excellent reason to crate train your Lab from the start. If he's a chewer, confine him to his crate with a legal chewy toy or bone anytime you can't watch him. I don't recommend that you make a regular practice of crating your dog up for extended periods. If you have to be gone longer than four or five hours on a regular basis, perhaps you can have someone come in during the day to exercise him for a little while. Many pet sitters offer such a service. If that's not possible, a portable dog run with a roof would give your dog more room to move around and access to a potty area while keeping him from chewing things he shouldn't. If you choose to leave him outside in a dog run, though, be sure he doesn't take up recreational barking. Ask your neighbors whether your dog is barking too much while your gone. If so, please find an alternative to leaving him outdoors, for everyone's well being.

When you are with your dog, keep him in the same room with you and keep an eye on him. If he picks up something he's not allowed to have, take it from him gently and give him one of his chewy toys. It may take your dog a while to learn what he can and can't have, but if you're patient and persistent, he will learn.

Don't Beg

Most people don't want a 70 pound dog staring at them while they eat, so teach your puppy not to beg–or more accurately, don't teach your puppy to beg. If you give your puppy a bit of what you're eating when he stares at you with that "Feed the Dog" look on his face, you teach him that the staring and begging behavior works. That's true whether he stares at you at the dinner table, or when you're munching chips on the couch. If you want to share a little with him (and please–not much! Labs are very prone to obesity), take him to another area (perhaps the kitchen) after you finish eating, have him do something (sit, lie down, a trick) and give him just a teensy bit. In the meantime, he should lie down and mind his own business, not stare at you and drool on your shoe.

Don't fall for the begging dog trick unless you plan to give in every time.

OK, I confess, I'm not really that tough. I do share this and that with my dogs–but not every time I eat, and not until I'm finished. I make them lie down and be polite while they wait–I don't like to feel I have to guard my grub from opportunistic canines. When I've finished and am ready to share, I take the dogs away from where I eat and have them do something to earn their share–sit, lie down, whatever. That way they get a little something. But not as a reward for begging. So share a little if you like (after all, this is your best friend we're talking about), but on your terms. Just remember that you should be the one in control. Don't let yourself be hypnotized by those big brown eyes.

Stop Pulling!

Walking your dog should be a safe, pleasant activity for both of you. But Labs are big, strong dogs, and all too many of them never learn to walk nicely on leash. There's nothing fun about being hauled along by a barely controlled dog. Aside from being frustrating and exhausting, your lack of control can actually endanger both you and your dog.

When out for a walk with your Lab, you are the one in control. Pulling is not allowed.

If you're starting to train a puppy, or your dog is easy to control, try the "no forward progress" approach first. Your dog pulls because he wants to move along faster, so teach him that pulling gets him the opposite of what he wants. Stop and stand still. It may take him a few seconds to realize that you're no longer moving, but that's okay. As soon as he stops pulling, praise him and start walking again. If he starts pulling again, stop in your tracks. You may not get far the first few times, but if your dog is a moderate puller, this may be enough to stop him in a few "stop and go" sessions.

If "stop and go" doesn't work, instead of stopping where you are, hold the leash with both hands in front of your waist, and turn and change directions. Don't wait for your dog, just turn and walk quickly in a different direction. Don't talk to him or jerk him–just go. When he catches up with you, praise him. You can give him a treat occasionally if you like to spark his interest. Most dogs quickly learn to stop pulling and to pay attention.

Some Labs are so used to pulling, and so strong and "enthusiastic," that you may need different equipment to give you better control, especially if you aren't big and strong yourself. Head halters work well on some Labs, but not all. Many people use pinch collars effectively and humanely on Labs. If you choose one of these training tools to gain better control, make sure that it fits your dog properly and that you understand how to use it properly. Used wrongly, any training device can be ineffective or even dangerous, so if you are inexperienced or uncertain, ask your obedience instructor for guidance. If you aren't

Excessive barking can be a problem.

taking an obedience class, consider doing so, or at least taking a few private lessons with a competent instructor. Halters and collars are simply tools–you still need to train your dog if you want to have the best possible control and a positive relationship.

Bark, Bark, Bark!

Barking is one of several vocal methods of communication used by dogs. A bark can be a warning, a complaint, a greeting, or an invitation to play. Labs are not generally nuisance barkers, but some are, particularly if bored, lonely, or under-exercised. Some Labs also bark to order people around. If your dog learns that barking gets him what he wants, then he may bark to be let out or in, or to get you to feed him, walk him, play with him. A little barking is normal, and can be useful as a "heads up" to let you know there's someone or something that you should be aware of. But a dog that barks and barks and barks, or a dog that barks at just about anything, is a nuisance.

Excessive barking is difficult to stop because it's a self-rewarding behavior–the dog gets pleasure from the act itself. But you can reduce nuisance barking with time and effort. If your Lab barks excessively, the first thing you need to do is figure out why he barks so much. Does he spend too much time alone? Is he bored? Does he have frequent stimulation to bark from things he sees or hears in his environment? Does he have separation anxiety? Is he aggressive? Aggression is not normal or desirable in a Lab, but some individuals do have aggression problems. Is he highly territorial? Some dogs bark at anyone or anything that comes near.

If your dog seems to be barking because he's lonely or bored, you may need to give him what he wants–on your terms. Remember–dogs are social animals, and Labs are particularly fond of spending time with their people. If you have to leave your dog alone a lot, be sure you spend lots of quality time with him when you are home. It's not enough to come home, pat his head, feed him, toss him outside to "exercise," and bring him in to go to sleep. You need to be sure he gets enough exercise *every day*. Spend time playing with

Part 3

him, grooming him, and petting him. If you haven't taken him to an obedience class, do it now. Even if he doesn't bark in class and you don't work directly on the problem, basic training frequently helps behavior in general. And if loneliness and boredom are at the root of the barking, spending time with you in class and practicing outside of class will help relieve both.

Boredom and lack of attention can lead to problem behaviors.

If your dog is territorial about your house, yard, and maybe your car, and is barking to warn away what he sees as intruders, obedience training will help. When your dog starts to bark at someone, give him another command and make sure he obeys. "Down" is particularly useful for this, because lying down puts your dog in a submissive position, which gives you control over the barking. Most dogs don't bark when they're lying down on command.

A number of "bark collars" supposedly designed to stop nuisance barking are available. They work by administering a "correction" in the form of an electrical shock, a spray aimed at the dog's nose (citronella is commonly used because dogs don't like the smell), or a high-pitched sound that hurts the dog's ears. Bark collars may seem like an easy solution to problem barking, but they don't do anything to alleviate the cause of the barking. The dog may learn not to bark, but since the stimulus is probably still there he may take up some equally annoying hobby like digging or chewing. If your dog is barking to defend his territory, he may think whoever he's barking at causes the correction from the collar, and he may become downright aggressive. If he barks because he's afraid or nervous, a bark collar will frighten him more. All in all, you're better off removing the cause of the barking if possible and providing your Lab with proper exercise, training, and attention.

Digging

Lots of Labs love to dig in the ground. Why do dogs dig?

• It's something to do! If your dog is left out by himself and gets bored, he may take up landscaping as a fun new pastime. Make sure he gets lots of daily exercise and stimulation,

Destructive digging can be prevented if you give your Lab a place where he can dig.

and don't leave him alone in your yard for long periods of time.

• To find buried treasure! Maybe there's a nest of underground creatures just waiting to be dug up. Or maybe he just thinks there is. Have you used bonemeal or blood meal in a garden? They smell like prey to your dog.

• To keep a secret! Some dogs really do bury things for safekeeping.

• To escape! If your dog is bored inside the yard, he may try to dig under the fence to see what's happening out there. Once again, work to prevent boredom. You can also secure the perimeter of your fence.

• To chill! On hot days, many dogs dig themselves a nice little bed in the cooler soil. Make sure your dog has a cool, shady spot and plenty of fresh, cool water if he's outdoors in warm weather.

• It's fun! Some dogs just like to dig holes.

One way to keep a serious digger from turning your yard into a moonscape is to give him his own place to dig. Pick a place, preferably in the shade, with loose sand or sandy soil (it's cleaner than clay or loam). If necessary, build a doggy sandbox for digging. Bury a treat or toy in the sand and bring your dog to the area. When he notices the scent of the treat or toy, encourage him to find it. If he doesn't get the idea, dig a little with your hands to help him get started. Do this for a few days. Don't let your dog be outside unsupervised, and if he starts to dig somewhere else, tell him, "Leave it," and take him to his spot. He'll figure it out.

There are other ways to discourage digging as well. No method works with every dog, but these methods all work on some dogs. If your dog digs in one particular spot, you may be able to discourage him by filling in his hole with rocks or concrete. I stopped my Lab, Raja, from digging up one section of a flower garden by putting chicken wire down and covering it with about three inches of soil. He didn't like getting his nails caught on that darned wire, and he stopped the digging.

Some people swear by various substances to discourage digging. Black pepper sprinkled on the area discourages some dogs, and certainly makes them sneeze. Mothballs repel most dogs, but they're toxic and may repel you, too. Pet supply stores sell products that are supposed to stop dogs from digging. The trouble with all these methods, though, is that they don't address the motivation and they don't provide an alternative. As with barking, if your Lab was digging because he was bored, he'll just find something else to do, and chances are you won't like it any more than you liked his digging. Retraining and redirecting energy, and a legal place to dig, are the best solutions.

Separation Anxiety

If your Lab gets very agitated and worried whenever he thinks you're leaving him, and if he barks, howls, salivates, paces the floor, or rips things up while your gone, he may have "separation anxiety." To deal with separation anxiety, you need to make sure your dog and your belongings are safe when you leave, and you need to address the anxiety itself. Crate train your dog and crate him when you go out. Most dogs feel safe in their crates once they're used to them. Give him a safe chewy toy so he'll have something to do to relieve the stress.

A chew toy and your calm attitude will keep your pup from being anxious when you're gone.

To help your dog get past the anxiety, begin by teaching him the "stay" command. Have him stay for varying lengths of time, working gradually up to half an hour or longer. Praise and reward him for staying put and relaxing. This will teach him that he doesn't have to follow you around and be beside you every single second. Have him spend some time in his crate even when you're home, and feed him in his crate so that he learns that the crate is a safe, wonderful place to be, no matter what.

When you leave and come home, don't make a fuss over your dog. Doing so tells him that he's right, your absence really is a big deal. Instead, put him in his crate with his toy while you're preparing to leave to give him a chance to relax. When you're ready to go, give him some special treat that he loves but gets only when you're gone––a hollow bone or chew toy stuffed with liverwurst, cheese, or peanut butter, for example. Ignore him when he's in his crate. You might leave a radio on softly. When you return, don't let your dog out of his crate immediately. Let him settle down, then quietly release him from the crate and take him out to potty. Keep things low key for a while, and then have a good playtime as a reward for being calm. Act like your comings and goings are no big deal.

You can help the situation, too, by using reconditioning exercises on days when you don't have to leave for long periods. Try to figure out how long you can be gone before your dog gets upset. Try leaving for shorter stretches than his critical limit. If he starts barking when you've been gone two minutes, walk out for one minute, then come back calmly and quietly. If your dog stayed relaxed, wait a few minutes and then let him out of the crate. If he acted anxious, stay close by but ignore your dog until he relaxes. Then reward him by letting him out, but don't make a fuss.

You may be able to help your anxious dog in others ways, too. Try to figure out what makes him relax. If he likes to look out the window, position his crate where he can see out if possible. If that makes him more anxious, put the crate in a more secluded spot. Soft music and talk help some dogs relax, so you might want to leave a radio on low. Some dogs like to have a little "memento" of their owner–maybe an old sweatshirt with your smell on it. Raja always took one of my walking shoes to his bed when I was gone. He never chewed it; he just liked to have it. For a dog, it's a sort of olfactory snapshot to remind him of the one he loves.

If you have to be gone long hours, try to have someone come in once or twice to give your dog a break. If your dog knows he won't be all alone for so long, he may not worry so much. Just getting out to potty rather than having to "hold it" for nine or ten hours could be a big help!

If you can't lessen or cure your dog's separation anxiety, seek help from your veterinarian or a qualified animal behaviorist. If nothing else works, you might try an anti-anxiety medication to break the cycle, but drugs are not a good solution for the long haul. A knowledgeable professional can help you evaluate your dog's situation and set up an effective treatment plan to relieve both you and your dog.

Mouthing and Biting

Labrador Retrievers are very interested in putting things in their mouths. Of course they are–they were designed to carry birds. Carrying things just feels good to them. Unfortunately, you may not appreciate having your Lab take your hand or forearm in his mouth, even if he does it gently.

Stop interacting with your dog when he begins to mouth you. Say, "Ow!", move out of reach, and ignore him for a minute or so. Then come back and resume what you were doing before. If he puts his mouth on you, ignore him again. Most dogs will quickly get the idea. If your dog persists, up the ante–leave him completely alone for a minute or so. Then return. It may take a few repetitions, but if you keep at it, he'll quit mouthing you.

Labs like to put things in their mouths. Have chew toys available for proper chewing.

Aggressive biting is entirely different from mouthing. If your Lab puppy or dog bares his teeth at you or anyone else, or snaps, or guards his food, toys, bed, or anything else from you, ask your veterinarian or obedience instructor for a referral, and talk to an experienced dog trainer or behaviorist who is qualified to deal with aggression. In any case, don't wait for the behavior to go away on its own. It won't. If your dog threatens you, take him seriously and get help immediately. You should also talk to your dog's breeder–aggressive behavior is not normal for a Labrador Retriever.

Correcting the Need to Chew

Labs, like all dogs, love to chew and put things in their mouths. Unless you don't mind your dog chewing on your new shoes or the corner of the couch, you need to redirect all of this chewing energy. Provide your Lab with a variety of chew toys, such as those made by Nylabone®. Rotate the toys that your Lab has to choose from to prevent boredom.

Aggression

Aggression in dogs can be caused by a number of things. Labrador Retrievers should have outgoing, stable temperaments, but a few don't–usually because of irresponsible breeding practices that didn't pay attention to temperaments in the breeding dogs. Some physical problems, such as hormonal imbalance or chronic pain, can also cause behavioral changes, including

Aggression in any dog should be treated with caution.

aggression. Some aggressive dogs direct their hostility at people, some at other animals, some at anything that moves. An aggressive dog–one that threatens to bite, tries to bite, or does bite–is dangerous. Keep in mind that because of his size, a Labrador Retriever that bites can cause serious injury, including broken bones. If your Lab behaves aggressively, you need to get qualified professional help *immediately*.

Start by having your vet give your dog a thorough physical exam. Be sure she knows about the aggression, for her own safety and so that she knows what she's looking for. Have her run a full thyroid panel (not just a thyroid screening)–low thyroid sometimes causes aggressive behavior. Improper levels of estrogen and testosterone can also cause aggressive behavior. Ask your vet about other tests you may want to have run. If a physical cause is found, it may be possible to treat it effectively, or it may not. At least you'll know why your dog is acting this way. Altering (spaying or castrating) cuts down on aggression if it's done before the dog reaches sexual maturity. In the end, though, if your dog remains aggressive you may have to consider having him euthanized. If your Lab is aggressive, please don't let him hurt anyone.

Part Four

Getting Active With Your Labrador Retriever

"I know you like the water, but do you always have to splash?"

8

Fun With Your Labrador Retriever

The Labrador Retriever is truly a versatile breed. If, like many people who share their lives with Labs, you find that you really enjoy the time you spend training your dog, you might want to consider some of the following activities. Whether you do it for competition, or just for fun, training will help build the bond between you and your dog. It will also help channel some of that joyful Labrador exuberance into safe, nondestructive, and even productive activity.

Training and competing in dog sports are a great way for you to spend time with your Lab.

Competitive Activities

Obedience

Obedience training and competition is a sport at which Labs do well. However, it is vital to realize

Titles Awarded By The American Kennel Club (AKC)

Titles Appearing Before a Dog's Name

Ch.—Champion (Conformation)

FC—Field Champion (Field Trial)

AFC—Amateur Field Champion

NAFC—National Amateur Field Champion

NFC—National Field Champion

OTCh.—Obedience Trial Champion

DC—Dual Champ (Ch. & FC)

TC—Triple Champ (Ch., FC, & OTCh.)

CGC—Canine Good Citizen®. This title is not officially recognized and will not appear on registration papers or pedigrees.

Titles Appearing After a Dog's Name

CD—Companion Dog

CDX—Companion Dog Excellent

UD—Utility Dog

UDX—Utility Dog Excellent

TD—Tracking Dog

TDX—Tracking Dog Excellent

VST—Variable Surface Tracker

JH—Junior Hunter

SH—Senior Hunter

MH—Master Hunter

NA—Novice Agility

NAJ—Novice Agility Jumper

OA—Open Agility

OAJ—Open Agility Jumper

AX—Agility Excellent

AXJ—Agility Excellent Jumper

MX—Master Agility

MXJ—Master Agility Jumper

that Labs need positive, upbeat training methods to remain happy in obedience work. The top obedience Labs are trained with fun and positive reinforcement and lots of variety in the training.

Labrador Retrievers are eligible to compete and earn obedience titles in several registries. The American Kennel Club (AKC) offers titles from the CD (Companion Dog) through the CDX (Companion Dog Excellent) and UD (Utility Dog) to the UDX (Utility Dog Excellent) and OTCh. (Obedience Trial Champion). To be eligible, your Labrador Retriever must be registered with the AKC. If your dog does not have registration papers, but is purebred and altered, you can obtain an Individual Limited Privileges (ILP) number in order to participate in performance events, including obedience.

The author and her Lab being awarded the CD title in Obedience.

The United Kennel Club (UKC) also offers an obedience titling program. To participate, your Lab must be UKC registered. You can get a Single Registration Application for your dog directly from the UKC. Competitors can earn the U-CD (United Companion Dog), the U-CDX, and the U-UD. In addition to its regular obedience program, the UKC offers an annual "Top Gun" International Obedience Competition.

The Australian Shepherd Club of American (ASCA) also opens its obedience competition to all breeds and mixed breeds and offers the ASCA CD, CDX, UD, and OTCh. To participate, your Labrador Retriever must be registered with one of the major registries (AKC, UKC, or the Canadian Kennel Club) and must have a Recording Number with ASCA.

One nice thing about obedience is that you can set your own goals. If you're the competitive type, you can go for high scores, High In Trial awards, and national honors. Or you can be satisfied simply to enjoy going in the ring with your dog, achieving your qualifying scores, and obtaining the dog's titles. Whatever your goals, get a copy of the obedience rulebook and read the rules of the individual obedience program before you enter your dog in a trial.

Agility

Agility is the fastest growing canine sport in the world, and lots of Labs are participating. In agility, the dog jumps, runs through tunnels, and negotiates other obstacles in proper order and style and within a set time. You can do agility just for fun with simple homemade equipment, or you can enter competition to earn titles and other honors. As in obedience, you set the goals that suit you and your dog.

Most agility instructors require that dogs have some basic obedience before starting an

Agility is growing in popularity around the world.

Titles Awarded by the Labrador Retriever Club (LRC)

WC—Working Certificate

WCX—Working Certificate Excellent

CC—Conformation Certificate

Labs may also earn conformation, hunt test and trial, obedience, agility, flyball, tracking, and therapy titles through a number of other registries.

agility class. Your dog must be responsive to you and must not interfere with other dogs and handlers. It is also important to let your puppy mature before jumping him or encouraging other actions that stress young bones and joints, which are more easily injured than their mature counterparts.

Several organizations sponsor agility competition. The rules, procedures, and obstacles vary somewhat among the organizations, so be sure to read the appropriate rulebook before entering your dog in competition.

The AKC offers the Novice Agility (NA), Novice Agility Jumpers (NAJ), Open Agility (OA), Open Agility Jumpers (OAJ), Agility Excellent (AX), Agility Excellent Jumpers (AXJ), and Master Agility Excellent (MX), Master Agility Excellent Jumpers (MXJ) titles. If a dog earns the AX title and then earns qualifying scores in the Agility Excellent class at ten licensed or member agility trials, he earns the Master Agility Excellent title (MX). The MXJ is achieved when the dog earns ten qualifying scores after earning the AXJ.

The United States Dog Agility Association (USDAA) offers eight agility titles. An Agility Dog® (AD) has had three clear rounds (no faults) under two different judges in the Starters or Novice class. An Advanced Agility Dog® (AAD) has had three clear rounds under two different judges in the Advanced class. The Master Agility Dog® (MAD) has demonstrated versatility with three clear rounds under two different judges in the Masters standard agility class and a qualifying score at the masters level in each of the following: Gamblers Competition, to show proficiency in distance control and handling; Pairs or Team Relay, to show cooperative team effort and good sportsmanship; Jumping Class, to show jumping ability and fluid working habit; and Snooker Competition, to show a dog and handler's versatility in strategic planning. To earn the Jumpers Master, Gamblers Master, Snooker Master, or Relay Master a dog must have five clear rounds in the appropriate class. A USDAA Agility Dog Champion has earned the Master Agility Dog, Snooker Master, Gamblers Master, Jumpers Master, and Relay Master titles. The USDAA also recognizes the Agility Top Ten annually.

This Lab is learning to negotiate the teeter for agility.

The USDAA promotes competition through tournament event, including its Grand Prix of Dog Agility championships. USDAA also has sponsors the Dog Agility Masters® team pentathlon championship to promote agility as a team sport and the $4,000 Dog Agility Steeplechase championship to demonstrate speed in performance. Dogs must be registered with the United States Dog Agility Association in order to compete in USDAA events.

The USDAA also offers special programs for older dogs and the younger handlers. The Veterans Program is for dogs seven years of age or older. The Junior Handler Program, designed to encourage young people to participate in dog agility as a fun, recreational family sport, is for handlers 18 years of age and under.

The North American Dog Agility Council (NADAC) offers Certificates of Achievement for the Regular, Jumpers, and Gamblers' classes. The Regular Agility Class is designed to show the handler and dog's ability to perform all of the agility obstacles safely and at moderate speed. The Open level classes test the handler and dog's ability to perform the obstacles at faster speeds with more directional and distance control and obstacle discrimination. The Elite level classes require more complex handler strategies and more speed from the dog.

Sucess in competition comes from training and teamwork.

A dog may be entered in the Standard Division, the Veterans Division, or the Junior Handlers Division. In all divisions, certification in the Regular Agility Classes requires three qualifying rounds under at least two different judges. NADAC awards the Agility Trial Champion (NATCh.) title to dogs that have earned a minimum of 200 points in the Regular Agility Classes at the Elite level after earning an Elite Agility Certificate; 100 points in the Gamblers classes at the Elite level after earning a Gamblers Certificate-Elite; and 100 points in the Jumpers classes at the Elite level after earning a Jumpers Certificate-Elite.

Flyball

Flyball, invented in California in the late 1970s, gets most dogs really excited. Participants run relay races as teams of four. Each team member runs down a lane over a series of four jumps spaced ten feet apart, hits a peddle on a spring-loaded box to release a tennis ball, grabs the ball, and runs back over the jumps. When the dog crosses the starting line, the next dog goes. The winner is the team whose four dogs finish first without errors.

The North American Flyball Association (NAFA) governs Flyball Competition in North America.

Each dog earns points towards his flyball titles based on the team's time. Titles are Flyball Dog (FD), Flyball Dog Excellent (FDX), Flyball Dog Champion (FDCh.), Flyball Master (FM), Flyball Master Excellent (FMX), Flyball Master Champion (FMCh.), and Flyball Grand Champion (FGDCh.).

Musical Freestyle

Musical freestyle combines dog obedience and dance into a lovely display of teamwork and rapport between dog and handler. Handlers wear costumes and sometimes the dogs do as well. The pair interprets a piece of music with their choreographed movements. Teamwork between the handler and dog is the focus, and both partners are judged.

Musical Canine Sports International (MCSI), the sport's only title-granting organization, awards titles in musical freestyle. On-leash and Off-leash divisions offer Individual (one handler, one dog), Brace, (two handlers, two dogs), and Team (three or more handlers, each with a dog) competition at three levels. Dogs that earn qualifying scores in the appropriate classes are awarded the titles MFD (Musical Freestyle Dog), MFX (Musical Freestyle Excellent), and MFM (Musical Freestyle Master). MCSI members sometimes hold seminars where you can get started in the sport.

In tracking, your Lab does what comes naturally: he follows his nose.

Tracking

Tracking is an activity in which your dog just does what comes naturally–he follows his nose. You just have to teach him to follow the track you want him to follow.

The AKC offers titles for registered dogs trained to track, and even if you don't want to pursue a title, training your Lab to track can be great fun, provide exercise for you and your dog, and give you the opportunity to observe the incredible powers of the Labrador nose. The best way to train is with other people and their dogs, and if you can find a tracking club, all the better. Some obedience clubs also have groups of people who enjoy training their dogs to track. Tracking as a sport is very time intensive and requires physical stamina, since you have to follow your dog. It's also a lot of fun.

Tracking Tests, which are not competitive, are designed to demonstrate the dog's ability to recognize and follow human scent. Before you can enter your dog in a Tracking Test, you must obtain a written statement signed by an AKC-approved tracking test judge certifying that your dog has passed a certification test within one year prior to the date the Tracking Test is to be held. The certification test should be equal in difficulty to an actual Tracking Test/TD.

A dog that passes two licensed or member club Tracking Tests under two judges earns the Tracking Dog (TD) title. A Tracking Dog Excellent (TDX) has passed two Tracking Dog

If planning on showing your dog, consult the breed standard to make sure your Lab

Excellent Tracking Tests, and the Variable Surface Tracking (VST) is awarded after the dog successfully completes the Variable Surface Tracking Test. The AKC Champion Tracker title is awarded to a dog who earns all three tracking titles.

Conformation

In conformation–what most people think of as a dog show class–the dog is judged against the breed standard. The original purpose of conformation shows was to assess the quality of potential breeding stock, and AKC conformation is still open only to intact animals.

In conformation, each breed is first judged by itself. The dogs (males) of each breed are judged first, then the bitches (females). A Winners Dog and Winners Bitch are chosen, and these are the animals that get points toward their championships. The Winners Dog and Bitch are judged once more against "specials"–Labs who already have their championships–for Best of Breed. At an all-breed show, the Best of Breed winner moves on to the Sporting Group and competes there against the Best of Breed winners from the other sporting breeds. Four dogs are selected in each group and placed in order. The winners of all the groups then compete for Best in Show.

In the US, Labs are eligible to compete in conformation at shows sanctioned by the American Kennel Club (AKC), the United Kennel Club (UKC), the States Kennel Club (SKC), or the International All Breed Kennel Club of America (IABKC). If you like to travel, your Lab can also compete in Canada, Mexico, and abroad. The rules and procedures for earning championships vary in the different registries so be sure to read the rules, and if possible watch a show or two before you enter your dog.

If you think you'd like to try conformation, be sure that the breeders you speak to know that. If you already have a Lab that you think you'd like to show but that you didn't buy for that purpose, talk to your breeder first. If your breeder didn't sell the dog as a show

LRC Conformation Certificate

In 1998, the LRC announced a new program for conformation evaluation open to all Labrador Retrievers. The Conformation Certificate is noncompetitive and is awarded to any Lab that passes an LRC-sanctioned conformation examination conducted by a judge approved by the AKC to judge Labrador Retrievers in conformation. Certificate evaluations are held in conjunction with field, obedience, and agility trials and hunt tests.

Dogs are judged according to the breed standard. The judge evaluates each dog as pass or fail on 14 conformation and temperament categories. A dog must have a 70-percent pass rate in all categories or at least 10 passing scores overall. Dogs with disqualifying faults will not receive the certificate. Although the Conformation Certificate is not an official title, it presents an opportunity for owners to have their dogs evaluated and to learn from those evaluations.

prospect, it may be that he has a fault that will hurt him in the ring. Study the breed standard and go through it point by point, evaluating your dog for each. If you can, have someone who is knowledgeable about Labrador Retriever conformation evaluate your dog with you. Or take your dog through a conformation certificate exam at an LRC event. Remember, too, that whether or not your Lab is show-quality has nothing to do with his quality as a topnotch companion!

If your dog has show potential train him for the show ring.

If your dog has potential as a show dog, you need to train him before you show him. Showing a dog in the conformation ring is harder than it looks. Contact your local Lab club, kennel club, or other training clubs to find out about conformation handling classes in your area. Go to dog shows and watch. Observe what the good handlers do to make their dogs look good. Read about handling–there are a number of excellent books on the market, and many magazines publish articles on handling.

If you can, go to some shows with an experienced Labrador Retriever exhibitor. You can offer to help in exchange for lessons on grooming and showing. A good mentor is worth her weight in entry forms!

When you're ready to give showing a whirl, consider starting with "matches" in your area. Wins at matches don't count toward championships, but matches let you practice your handling and let your dog get used to the ring environment without the pressure of a real show.

For Fun and Fellowship

Labs are people-loving, fun-loving dogs, and some of the best things you can do with your Lab are noncompetitive activities that let you both enjoy the fundamental pleasures of the canine-human partnership. Let's look at a few that are particularly good for Labs and Lab people.

A therapy dog needs to have basic obedience skills, be well mannered, and be under excellent control.

Dog-Assisted Therapy

The Labrador Retriever's natural love for people makes it an ideal candidate for therapy work. Therapy dogs work in all sorts of environments. Lots of them visit nursing homes and hospices, brightening the lives of the residents, many of whom miss the dogs they had in their earlier lives. Therapy dogs and their handlers work in many other environments, too, including hospitals, schools and residential programs for handicapped children, mental health environments, physical rehabilitation facilities, children's homes, women's and children's shelters. Therapy dogs have even been used at disaster sights to provide relief for victims and rescue workers who just need to hug a dog.

To qualify as a therapy dog, your Lab will have to have basic obedience skills and be well-mannered and under excellent control. He must honestly like people of all kinds and must be reliable and calm around odd noises, smells, and activities.

A number of organizations offer training and certification for Therapy Dogs, and therapy visitation groups exist throughout the country. Therapy Dogs, Incorporated, certifies dog-and-handler teams based on a basic test and several observations of the team at work in a therapy setting. Therapy Dogs International, Inc., uses a modified form of the AKC's Canine Good Citizen® (CGC) test to determine whether a dog is suitable for therapy work. The Delta Society offers several different types of certification. Some local organizations also offer certification. You and your Lab can also make therapy visits without being certified, but certification offers some advantages: you and your dog have more credibility, you're usually covered by insurance while working in a therapy environment, and certifying organizations usually offer some measure of support and training. The rewards of therapy work are less tangible than ribbons won in competition, but they are every bit as real. And what better way could there be to share with the world the love that shines from deep, dark eyes framed in a sweet Labrador face?

Hiking and Backpacking

Getting out and about in the open air is a lot more fun with a friend, and Labs are naturals. Your dog can learn to wear a backpack (but do build him up slowly to carrying weight). He can carry his own food and water, and if you help him a bit he can be a good citizen and carry his feces back in a baggy for proper disposal so that public areas will continue to be open to well-mannered dogs and their responsible owners.

By Paw and Foot

Walking, jogging, or running are great ways to keep you and your Lab in shape. Before you start a jogging program, be sure your dog's nails are trimmed, his pads are in good condition, and he's not too much overweight. Start slowly and build up. If possible, jog mostly on soft surfaces like dirt trails or grass; pavement is harder on your dog's joints, and in summer it can be very hot for his foot pads. If you're new to a serious exercise program, physical checkups for both of you may be in order before you start.

9

Working Your Lab as a Retriever

I can't explain what it feels like to watch a dog's instinct kick in as he does the work he was born to do, but believe me, it's wonderful. Generation upon generation of Labrador Retrievers have been selected by breeders and owners for their ability and desire to seek and find game birds in icy water or rough terrain, and to return the birds to the hands of their human partners.

Training Your Lab to Work in the field is a rewarding experience.

Tossing a ball or stick for a jolly Lab will give you a hint of the real thing, but if you want a thrill, take your Lab to the field. Even if you aren't interested in hunting or competing with your dog, you can participate in field training and practice to develop and satisfy your Lab's natural instincts. If

The Lab must be trained to complete retrieves on land

Before You Get a Lab for Hunting

Hunting season in most areas lasts only a few weeks, but dogs are year-round. Before you get a Lab for hunting, be sure you also want him as a companion and friend. Even if he lives with the most dedicated of sportsmen, most of a hunting Lab's hours will be spent doing something other than hunting or training. A hunting dog is not just another piece of equipment that can be put aside until next season. Every dog deserves love, activity, companionship, and social contact every day throughout his life.

you would like to put titles on your dog to prove his abilities, you might train for and enter hunt tests or field trials, too.

Hunting With Your Labrador Retriever

Many Labrador Retrievers still accompany and assist hunters in the pursuit of waterfowl and upland game birds, and many hunters still consider the Labrador Retriever to be the consummate retrieving dog and companion in the field.

I can't explain the ins and outs of field training here–whole books, magazines, and video tapes are devoted to that. There are also many local and national organizations, as well as private trainers, devoted to training and using Labs and other retrievers for hunting. Your best bet is to consult your Lab's breeder or look for national and local clubs with an interest in retrievers.

Keep Your Lab in top condition if You want him to become a hunting companion.

Soundness in body and mind are essential in a good hunting dog. If you already have a Lab that you plan to use for hunting, keep him at a healthy weight, keep

Contacts for Field Training and Hunting Information

American Kennel Club (AKC)
AKC Headquarters
260 Madison Ave.
New York, NY 10016
(212) 696-8200
www.akc.org/dic/events/hunting/

The Labrador Retriever Club of America (LRC)
Secretary: Christopher G. Wincek
14686 Grand Army of the Republic Highway
Hambden, OH 44024
thelabradorclub.com/

National Labrador Retriever Club (NLRC)
Secretary and Newsletter Editor: Becky Jack
(425) 450-0742
nipntucklr@aol.com
labradorretrievers.org/

North American Hunting Retriever Association (NAHRA)
P.O. Box 5159
Fredericksburg, VA 22403
Phone: (540) 286-0625
Fax: (540) 286-0629
www.nahra.org/index.shtml

North American Versatile Hunting Dog Association (NAVHDA)
P.O. Box 520
Arlington Heights, IL 60006
Phone: (847) 253-6488
Fax: (847) 255-5987
Email: navoffice@aol.com
www.navhda.org/

his vaccines and other veterinary care up-to-date, and be sure he's properly exercised and conditioned before taking him to the field. Retrieving in cold water and over rough terrain is vigorous physical work. It's not fair to let your dog be a couch potato most of the year and then expect him to suddenly be an athlete.

If you're still deciding between pups and want a hunting Lab, look for a healthy pup or adult from an experienced breeder of hunting dogs (see Chapter 2). Look for a dog that likes to retrieve naturally, is outgoing and confident, and is not frightened of noises. Let the breeder help you choose–a good breeder knows more about the puppy or dog than you can possibly learn in an hour or so.

Encourage the natural behaviors that you want your puppy to develop. Never discourage your Lab from bringing you things! However, if you don't want your dress shoes toted around the house, put them away. If your dog finds them and brings you one, praise him

Get Your Lab used to the noise of a shooting gun to keep him from becoming gun-shy.

Most Labs love the water and take to it in no time.

and reward him, take the shoe, and replace it with something he is allowed to carry around. The last thing you want is a retriever who's afraid he'll get yelled at for retrieving.

Start your pup early with basic obedience training and stick with it. A hunting retriever needs to be very reliable on certain basic commands. He must stay when you tell him to and come when you call. He must learn to mark the fall of a shot bird and to follow your directions even when excited and distracted. A bird dog must also be steady and confident under fire, so accustom your hunting Lab to loud noises.

Most Labs do have a natural affinity for water, but don't force your dog into it. Give your pup time to test the waters–literally–on his own terms. Some puppies will rush right in and never look back. Others need to wade around and get used to the idea. Never throw a puppy into deep water–all that will accomplish is to teach him that you can't be trusted.

Some Field Terms

Birdy: A dog with a very high desire to retrieve birds.

Blind: A structure in which hunters hide themselves from game. In a field trial or hunt test, the gunner is hidden in a blind.

Blind retrieve: Test in which the dog does not see the bird fall and does not know where the bird is. The handler uses hand signals and voice and whistle commands to guide the dog to the bird.

Break: A dog breaks when he leaves to retrieve the bird before he's released by the handler.

Bumper (dummy): A canvas or plastic object used in retriever training to simulate a bird.

Cast: To send the dog in a specific direction after stopping him at a distance with the whistle.

Conditioned retrieve (forced retrieve): Training which teaches the dog to pick up, hold, and deliver objects on command.

Cover: Vegetation on land or in water that may hide a bird from a dog.

Field Trial: Competitive event for working retrievers.

Gunner: The person who throws and/or shoot the birds during training, hunt tests, or field trials.

Honor: A dog honors another dog by remaining in position while the other dog works. The honoring dog must not interfere with the working dog.

Hunt Test: Non-competitive event for working retrievers.

Mark: The fall of a bird. A working retriever is expected to mark, or watch, the fall of a shot bird, remember where it fell, and retrieve it when released to do so.

Quartering: Covering the ground systematically in search of game.

Steady: A dog is steady if it remains in position without physical restraint until sent to retrieve.

Style: A dog's manner of working.

Field Trials and Hunting Tests

If you're not interested in hunting but would like to participate in sports that utilize and develop your Lab's instincts and abilities, you might enjoy training for and participating in hunt tests or field trials. Check with the local affiliates of national clubs for more information.

Hunt Tests

Retriever Hunt Tests are non-competitive events designed to test the dog's instinct and ability to perform the tasks for which the Labrador Retriever was developed. Several organizations offer hunt tests for which Labs are eligible. The requirements for titles in the various organizations are outlined below.

The AKC offers Retriever Hunt Tests at three levels for all AKC-registered retrievers.

The American Kennel Club (AKC)

The AKC offers Retriever Hunt Tests at three levels for all AKC-registered retrievers and Irish Water Spaniels, including dogs with Limited Registration and Indefinite Listing Privilege (ILP) registration. A dog may be entered at any level for which it is trained, as it is not required to earn any title as a prerequisite for earning a higher title.

The Junior Hunter (JH) title requires the dog to earn qualifying scores in four AKC Junior Hunter Tests, in which the dog must successfully retrieve four single marks (fall birds): two on land and two in water.

Retrieving can be practiced at home with a Nylabone® Flexible FRISBEE® Flying Disc.

To earn the Senior Hunter (SH) title, an untitled dog must earn qualifying scores in five AKC Senior Hunting Tests. If the dog already has earned the JH title, then he needs four qualifying scores in Senior Hunter Tests, which include one blind retrieve on land, one blind retrieve on water, one double land mark, and one double water mark. In a double mark, two marks are presented before the dog is sent to retrieve, so the dog must remember two fallen birds.

To become a Master Hunter (MH), a dog with a SH title must earn qualifying scores in five AKC Master Hunting Tests. If the dog has not earned the SH, then he must earn qualifying scores in six Master Hunting Tests to be awarded the MH title. The Master Hunting Test tests the dog in at least five simulated hunting situations, including multiple land marks, multiple water marks, multiple marks on water and land, a blind retrieve on land, and a blind retrieve on water, of which at least one should be a double blind. Diversion birds and/or another diversion are used on at least one of the marks, and the test must include at least one double mark.

The AKC began its Retriever Hunting Test program in 1985.

The Labrador Retriever Club of America (LRC)

The LRC offers tests in which a qualifying dog earns a Working Certificate (WC) or a Working Certificate Excellent (WCX). To earn the Working Certificate, the dog must show that he is not gun-shy and must retrieve a shot game bird at a distance of 50 yards or more on land. He must also retrieve two ducks from water deep enough to require him to swim. The second retrieve comes immediately after the first to show the dog's willingness to reenter the water. The dog does not have to be steady on the line and may be lightly restrained prior to the retrieves. He does not have to deliver the bird to hand, but must bring it within a reasonable distance of his handler. A WC will also be awarded upon request to any dog that has accomplished one of the following: successfully completed both a land and water series in an AKC field trial; earned a placement or judge's award of merit in an AKC field trial; earned the AKC Junior Hunter (JH) Title, or at least one leg toward a Senior Hunter (SH) or Master Hunter (MH) Title.

Practice water retrieves whenever possible.

The purpose of the WC is to encourage owners and breeders of Labrador Retrievers to maintain the natural hunting and retrieving abilities in the dogs

In hunting tests, Labs compete for points toward titles rather than placement.

because those traits are considered genetically essential to the breed. The LRC considers this point so important that no member of the organization is allowed to use the title Ch. (conformation champion) in front of the name of an AKC-registered Labrador Retriever until the dog has received a WC or the equivalent as described above.

The Working Certificate Excellent (WCX) is intended to encourage the development of natural hunting and retrieving abilities through training. It requires a double mark on land and a double in water. The dog must deliver the bird to hand and must be steady on the line without restraint.

The Hunting Retriever Club (HRC)

The HRC, an affiliate of the United Kennel Club (UKC), offers Hunt Tests in which dogs earn points toward titles awarded by the UKC. The Hunting Retriever (HR) title is awarded to a dog that earns 40 Championship Points in hunt tests at the Started, Seasoned, and/or Finished levels. The title Hunting Retriever Champion (HRCh.) is awarded to a dog that earns 100 Championship Points, with at least 60 points earned at the Finished level. A dog that has earned the HRCh. becomes a Grand Hunting Retriever Champion (GRHRCh.) by earning an additional 200 points–80 of which must be earned from the Grand category. The title Upland Hunter (UH) is awarded to the dog that earns 40 Upland Hunter Championship Points.

You can start training your Lab to retrieve while he's still a puppy.

The test for Started Hunting Retrievers and Handlers is set up to replicate actual hunting conditions. Because the test is for young or inexperienced hunting retrievers, judges look for performance based on natural ability rather than intensive training. A Started Hunting Retriever must successfully complete two marked water retrieves and two marked land retrieves.

The test for Seasoned Hunting Retrievers and Handlers requires more training and control. They are judged on both style and natural ability. The dog must be steady on the line and must retrieve to hand in five tests. The test must include a double-marked land retrieve, a double-marked water retrieve, a walk-up or tracking or quartering test, a blind land retrieve, and a blind water retrieve. A diversion must be included in the test.

The test for Finished Hunting Retrievers evaluates style and accuracy as well as natural ability and training. The Finished Hunting Retriever must be steady and under control and must respond promptly to voice or whistle commands. The dog must successfully complete four tests, including a multiple marked water retrieve and a multiple marked land retrieve, at least one of which must include an honor and a diversion, a water blind retrieve, and a land blind retrieve. An upland game test may be included at the judge's discretion.

The North American Hunting Retriever Association (NAHRA)

NAHRA's stated mission is to promote the field testing of retrievers and to educate the public about the value of purebred retrievers as wildlife conservation animals. NAHRA affiliate clubs exist throughout the US.

To earn the title Started Retriever (SR), a dog must qualify four times in the Started tests. To earn the title Working Retriever (WR), a dog must earn 20 points in Intermediate tests. A dog must either qualify five times in Senior tests or four times in Senior tests if he already holds the Working Retriever title to become a Master Hunting Retriever (MHR). A dog that qualifies 15 times in Senior tests is designated Grand Master Hunting Retriever (GMHR).

Your Lab should be alert when out in the field. You should have his attention at all times.

NAHRA offers several special awards in addition to the basic hunt test titles. If a dog qualifies in four Started or four Intermediate tests between January 1 and December 31, he receives a Brass Band Award and is qualified to participate in a Started/Intermediate Regional Invitational Field Test. If a dog qualifies in five Senior tests within a year from May

Many local clubs offer field training. The author and her Lab (left) await their turn.

1 to April 30 or earns the Master Hunting Retriever, he is invited to attend the Richard A. Wolters/NAHRA Invitational Field Test.

The North American Versatile Hunting Dog Association (NAVHDA)

NAVHDA was organized to foster, improve, promote, and protect the versatile hunting dog in North America with an eye to assist in the conservation of wild game, prevent cruelty to animals, and help hunters train their dogs to work as effective hunting companions on land and in water. NAVHDA International oversees the activities of local chapters throughout the US and Canada, which sponsor the hunting dog training and testing programs.

NAVHDA tests are conducted in environments that reflect actual hunting conditions and situations common to the area. During regular tests, three judges evaluate the performance of each dog against a standard of performance. At the Invitational Test, dogs work with other dogs present in the field to demonstrate each animal's willingness around other dogs as they might in actual hunting conditions. Each dog that meets or exceeds the minimum standard in each area of work is awarded a Prize I (highest), II, or III, based on a numerical score.

In 1969, NAVHDA established a system of four types of comprehensive tests to evaluate the performance of versatile hunting dogs at different stages of maturity. NAVHDA makes its performance records for individual dogs available, seeing the information as vital to the decision-making processes of both breeders and buyers.

The Natural Ability Test evaluates the natural abilities of young dogs and assesses their potential as versatile gun dogs. Each dog is tested and rated on seven important abilities: nose, search, tracking, pointing, water, desire, and cooperation.

The Utility Preparatory Test measures a dog's development midway through his field training. The Utility Test evaluates the trained dog in the water and on land, before and after the shot, as a versatile hunting companion.

NAVHDA also invites "exceptional animals who have demonstrated a high level of training" to participate in the Invitational Test, which tests each dog's skills in advanced fieldwork. Only dogs that have earned a Prize I in Utility are invited.

Dual and Triple Champions

An AKC Dual Champion Labrador Retriever is one that has earned an AKC Field Championship (FCh.) and AKC Show Championship (Ch.). If the dog also earns an AKC Obedience Trial Championship (OTCh.), the dog is a "Triple Champion."

AKC Field Trials

Unlike hunt tests in which dogs do not compete against each other but are instead evaluated against a standard of performance, field trials are competitive events in which dogs compete against each other for honors in addition to meeting certain standard requirements to earn titles. In the US, field trials are part of the AKC's performance competition program. To earn top honors in AKC field trials requires dedication, talent, and training.

AKC-licensed retriever field trials are open to all AKC-registered retrievers and Irish Water Spaniels, including dogs with Limited Registrations. Dogs with Indefinite Listing Privilege (ILP) registration are not eligible for field trials.

The competition is set up in "stakes," or levels. Minor Stakes are the Qualifying and Derby. Major Stakes (which may be divided further into subdivisions) include the Open All-Age and Amateur All-Age.

In field trials, dogs compete for honors in addition to meeting requirements toward earning a title.

The Derby Stake is for retrievers under two years of age. At this level, the dog is expected to be reasonably steady and obedient, but marking ability and style are more important than control. Retrieves are usually single and double marks. Blind retrieves are not required. Usually there are four tests: two on land and two in water. "Derby Points" are awarded for placements, and the dog that accumulates the most Derby points nationally during his "Derby career" is designated the "High-Point Derby Dog" by

"Bumpers" are used in place of birds in most training.

Retriever Field Trial News (RFTN). Although that designation is not an official AKC award, it carries a lot of prestige among field trialers. *RFTN* also recognizes the "Top Ten Derby Dogs" and publishes the "Derby List" of dogs that accumulate ten or more Derby points.

The Qualifying Stake is open to any dog that has not won two Qualifying Stakes, has not received a Judges Award of Merit in an Open All-Age Stake, and has not placed in an Amateur All-Age Stake. A Qualifying Stake usually includes triple retrieves and blind retrieves.

Championship points are awarded in the Open All-Age Stake. Only an accomplished retriever of excellent natural ability and training will excel in the Open All-Age Stake. Tests commonly include triple or quadruple marks, with and without retired guns (a gunner who hides after the bird is shot) and single, double, or triple blind retrieves. The dog must be steady and controlled at all times. The dog that earns the most points in the Open All-Age Stake at AKC-Licensed Field Trials during the year wins the prestigious High-Point Open Dog Award.

Championship points toward the Amateur Field Championship (AFCh.) are awarded in the Amateur All-Age Stake, which has essentially the same requirements as the Open All-Age stake, except that only amateur handlers may handle dogs in the Amateur Stake, while professional handlers may handle dogs in the Open All-Age Stake. Some trials include an Owner-Handler Amateur All-Age Stake in which the dog must be handled by the registered owner (or certain relatives) and the handler must be an amateur. The dog that earns the most points in the Amateur All-Age Stake at AKC-Licensed Field Trials during the year wins the prestigious High-Point Amateur Dog Award.

The AKC awards several Field Trial Championships. To become a Field Champion (FC), a retriever must earn ten points in the Open All-Age Stake, of which five points must be for a first place. Championship points are awarded for placements in the Open All-Age and the Amateur All-Age Stakes as follows: First Place = five points; Second Place = three points; Third Place = two points; Fourth Place = a half-point.

The title Amateur Field Champion (AFCh.) is awarded for points earned in the Amateur All-Age Stakes and the Open All-Age Stake when the dog is handled by an amateur rather than a professional trainer/handler. To attain the title of AFCh., the dog must earn 15 points, of which 5 must be for a first place.

The AKC also sponsors the National Amateur Championship annually in June and the National Open Championship in November. To qualify for the National Open Retriever Championship or the National Amateur Retriever Championship, a dog must have a five-point win and earn two additional points during the preceding year. Qualifying points for National Amateur Retriever Championship must be earned in the Amateur All-Age Stake or the Open All-Age Stake if the handler is an amateur. For the National Open Retriever Championship Open, points may be earned in the Open All-Age Stake or the Amateur All-Age Stake.

10

Traveling With (and Without) Your Labrador Retriever

Labrador Retrievers love to go everywhere their people go, and most dog-lovers like to go places with their dogs. A few simple guidelines can keep car travel pleasant and safe for you and your Lab.

An unrestrained dog may be injured in an accident.

Car Travel

All-too-often we see grinning Labs hanging out car windows or riding loose in the backs of pickup trucks, ears flying, tongues lolling. That image of freedom and joy on the open road has lots of appeal. The trouble is that dogs that travel that way can be seriously injured or even killed. Bits of dust, insects, and other airborne debris can seriously injure eyes and ears when they hit at the speed of a moving vehicle. Many dogs each year

Securing Your Lab in a crate is the safest way for him to travel.

Did You Know?

Perhaps 80°F weather doesn't seem unreasonable to you, but on a sunny day, in a closed car, that temperature can soar to well over 100°F in a few minutes. In less than 30 minutes, the temperature could be heading toward 125°F. No dog could sustain these temperatures without suffering irreparable brain damage or deth.

jump out of moving vehicles. If a dog isn't killed or badly hurt when he hits the ground, he may be hit by another vehicle. If you think your dog really needs to feel the wind in his ears, buy him a fan, but please keep him safe when traveling.

The safest way for a dog to ride in a moving vehicle is in a secure crate. A crate will keep an excited Lab puppy from becoming a lap puppy while you're driving–not a safe maneuver for either of you. If you're involved in an accident, your dog is a lot safer in a crate than he is loose in the car or even in a safety harness. You don't want your dog to survive an accident only to be released into traffic when someone opens the car door (or a door springs open). A loose dog can easily be killed or lost in the confusion at an accident scene. If you happen to be injured, emergency personnel can get to you much more easily if your dog is crated rather than loose, especially if he decides he needs to protect you. If you're unconscious or unable to control your dog, and he's perceived as a threat, emergency personnel may have no choice but to disable him somehow–not a pleasant thought. All in all, dogs are safer riding in crates than loose. If your dog travels with you a lot, it's a good idea to attach information to the crate that identifies your dog and gives the name and telephone number of someone who will care for him in an emergency.

A doggy seatbelt is a dog harness made to fasten to your car's seatbelt to keep your dog from being thrown around in a quick stop or an accident. It's a reasonable alternative to a crate, at least for short trips. If you use a harness, or let your dog ride loose, never let him ride in the front seat of a vehicle with passenger side air bags. He could be killed or injured if an air bag deploys.

Finally, but maybe most important, never leave your dog alone inside a parked car for more than a few minutes–and not at all on a warm or hot day. Do you like to sit in a closed-up car when the outside temperature is even moderately warm? We all know that a closed car gets uncomfortably warm very quickly–in fact, it can become lethal in just a few minutes. If you won't be able to take your Lab out of the car with you, then he's better off safe at home.

Make sure your Lab has food and water when traveling by air.

Air Travel

Dogs fly around the US and abroad every year. They fly for competitive events, for breeding, to reach new homes, and to go with their people on vacations. If you want your Lab to fly somewhere, he'll have to travel as cargo unless he is still a very small puppy, in which case he may qualify to travel in the cabin. Dogs in the cabin must fit into a small carry-on crate that will fit under a seat, and puppies must be at least eight weeks old to fly on commercial airplanes, so the window of opportunity for Labs in the cabin is very narrow. Unless your Lab is a service dog or certified search and rescue dog, he'll fly cargo.

Each airline has its own regulations concerning flights with dogs, and as I write this the regulations are in a state of flux, so check with the airline you plan to use for booking requirements, prices, restrictions, and so on. Regardless of which airline you use, certain rules apply. The dog must be in an airline-approved crate that is large enough for the dog to stand, lie down, and turn around.

Dog Allowed?

Not all hotels and motels accept dogs. The days of traveling until you are exhausted and checking into the first hotel or motel you see are a thing of the past when your canine pal is accompanying you. There are some wonderful resources you can refer to that will help to avoid accommodation problems. It is wise to contact places you plan to visit well before you leave for your trip. Do your homework at *www.petswelcome.com.*

Your Lab must have a health certificate issued by a vet before traveling.

You must provide absorbent bedding in the crate, as well as water and food bowls. The dog must have a health certificate issued by a veterinarian within ten days prior to the flight. Airline personnel will inspect the inside as well as the outside of the crate prior to accepting your dog for transport.

Accommodations

Lots of motels and some bed and breakfasts and other facilities allow dogs, if you like to travel with your Lab. Unfortunately, some dog owners have been less-than-responsible about their dogs over the years, and some motels and other places no longer allow the rest of us to bring our best friends with us. We all need to be considerate when we go places with our dogs if we want to continue to find accommodations for the whole family when we travel.

Your dog's crate provides a home away from home when you travel.

Probably the biggest *faux pas* that people make is not cleaning up after their dogs. Labrador Retrievers have not-insignificant bowel movements, and leaving them around for other people to step in or otherwise encounter is the height of rudeness. It's easy enough to carry some plastic bags and to pick up after your dog and deposit his offerings in a waste receptacle. Male Labs do not need to mark the shrubbery or porch railings where we stay, and females don't need to decorate motel lawns with yellow circles.

Dogs shouldn't be left alone in motel rooms, even if they are crated and well-behaved. Even a reliable dog may bark or chew something in a strange place. When making reservations, check the motel's dog policy, even if you've found information in a published or online source. Policies change. Some motels charge a deposit or additional fee for doggy guests, so ask about charges and refund policies before you check in.

If your dog hasn't stayed in a motel before, bring his crate and let him sleep in it. It's a piece of home that will comfort him in this strange place.

Boarding Kennels

Sometimes our dogs just can't come along. When that's the case, one option is to board your dog at boarding kennel. Ask your veterinarian, your dog's obedience instructor, and your friends with dogs for recommendations. Check out the kennel well in advance. Ask for a tour of the facility. Kennel runs, walkways, and exercise areas should be secure and clean, and dogs should have clean water at all times. Your dog should have a kennel run to himself, unless you are boarding more than one dog and you want them to "room" together.

Be sure to check out any kennel where you might board you Lab.

Some kennels offer extra services, such as extra walks or play times, a bath before you pick your dog up, or in-house training during your dog's stay. Be sure you understand the basic services and the charges for those and any extras. Find out who will handle your dog, and what their qualifications are. Ask about security. Is the kennel area fenced so that if your dog slips out the door to his kennel run he'll still be confined and safe? What safeguards are there against theft or vandalism? What provisions are there for emergency veterinary care? Is there an effective evacuation plan in place in case of fire or other emergency? Is someone on site at night and on weekends? If you're not comfortable with the answers to any of these questions, take your dog somewhere else or hire a pet sitter.

A pet sitter can care for your Lab in the comfort of his own home.

Pet Sitters

A pet sitter who comes to your home to care for your dog, your other pets, and sometimes to perform other services such as watering plants and collecting mail and newspapers is often a good alternative to a boarding kennel. Ask your veterinarian, obedience instructor, and friends for recommendations. Check the sitter's references. Be sure the sitter is competent and that she and your Lab like each other. She should be bonded and have reliable transportation and the ability to get your dog to a veterinarian if necessary.

Resources

Organizations and Clubs

Labrador Retriever Club of America, Inc.

Corresponding Secretary
Mr. Christopher G. Wincek
2555 Som Center Road
Hunting Valley, Ohio 44022
(440) 473-5255
Rodarbal@aol.com

Breeder Contact
Jody M. Thomas
2 North Street
Angawam, MA 01001
(413) 789-5543
Chesrite@aol.com

Rescue National Coordinators
Kathleen and Ralph Natushko
Telephone: (248) 589-8529 (no calls after 10 pm Eastern time please)
Fax: 248-616-0724

Emergency Fund
The LRC maintains a National Fund for the emergency care of Labs who are abandoned in multiple numbers (for instance, during floods, tornadoes, death of owner, or puppy mill shut down). This fund was established to pay for immediate needs such as vaccinations, health checks, or short-term boarding. It is available to any organized Labrador Rescue Group that is recognized by the National Coordinator. If you would like to support this program, you may send a donation to;

Dudley Millikin, Jr.
Treasurer, LRC, Inc.
109 Holt Road
Andover, MA 01810

American Kennel Club

Headquarters:

260 Madison Avenue

New York, NY 1001

Operations Center:

5580 Centerview Drive

Raleigh, NC 27606-3390

Customer Services:

Phone: (919) 233-9767

Fax: (919) 816-3627

www.akc.org

American Kennel Club's Canine Good Citizen Program:

www.akc.org/love/cgc/index.cfm

American Kennel Club's National Breed Club Rescue Network:

www.akc.org/breeds/rescue.cfm

The Kennel Club

1 Clarges Street

London

W1J 8AB

Phone: 087 0606 6750

Fax: 020 7518 1058

www.the-kennel-club.org.uk

The Canadian Kennel Club

89 Skyway Avenue

Suite 100

Etobicoke, Ontario, Canada

M9W 6R4

Order Desk & Membership: 1-800-250-8040

Fax: (416) 675-6506

www.ckc.ca

The United Kennel Club, Inc.

100 E. Kilgore Road

Kalamazoo, MI 49002-5584

(616) 343-9020

www.ukcdogs.com

United States Dog Agility Association (USDAA)

PO Box 850955

Richardson, TX 75085-0955

(972) 231-9700

Information Line: (888) AGILITY

Website: *www.usdaa.com/*

Email: *info@usdaa.com*

Agility Association of Canada (AAC)

RR#2

Lucan, Ontario

N0N 2J0

(519) 657-7636

North American Dog Agility Council (NADAC)

11522 South Hwy 3

Cataldo, ID 83810

www.nadac.com

Canine Performance Events (CPE)

P.O. Box 445

Walled Lake, MI 48390

Email: *cpe-agility@juno.com*

Musical Freestyle

Musical Canine Sports International

Sharon Tutt, Treasurer/Membership Chair

16665 Parkview Place

Surrey, B.C., Canada

V4N 1Y8

Phone: (604) 581-3641.

Therapy

Therapy Dogs Incorporated

PO BOX 2786

Cheyenne, Wyoming 82003

(307) 638-3223

Therapy Dogs International, Inc.

88 Bartley Road

Flanders, NJ 07836

Phone: (973) 252-9800

Fax: (973) 252-7171

Email: *tdi@gti.net*

Website: *www.tdi-dog.org*

Delta Society Pet Partners Programs

289 Perimeter Road East

Renton, WA 98055

Phone (206) 226-7357

Website: *PETSFORUM.com/DELTASOCIETY/*

Love on a Leash

Liz Palika

3809 Plaza Dr. #107-309

Oceanside, CA 92056

Phone (619) 630-4824

Publications of Interest

Books on Labrador Retrievers

Robert J. Berndt and Richard L. Myers

The Labrador Retriever

William W. Denlinger, 1983.

Janet I. Churchill

The New Labrador Retriever

Howell Book House, 1995.

Carole Coode

The Labrador Retriever Today

Howell Book House, 1993.

Nancy Martin

The Versatile Labrador Retriever

DORAL Publishing, 1994.

Anna Katherine Nicholas
The Book of the Labrador Retriever
TFH Publications, 1983.

Mary Roslin-Williams
Advanced Labrador Breeding
H.F. & G. Witherby, Ltd., 1988.

Clarice Rutherford, Barbara Brandstad, and Sandra Whicker
Retriever Working Certificate Training
Alpine Publications, 1986.

Helen Warwick
The New Complete Labrador Retriever, 3rd Edition
Howell Book House, 1989.

Richard A. Wolters
The Labrador Retriever: The history...the people, new edition
Richard A. Petersen Prints, 1992.

Bernard Zeisso
The Labrador Retriever
TFH Publications, 1995.

Books on Rescuing Dogs and Adopting Rescued Dogs

Sheila W. Boneham, Ph.D
Breed Rescue: How to Start and Run a Successful Program
Alpine, 1998.
Copies ordered at *www.perennialaussies.com/book-page.html* earn money for Labrador rescue.

Bob Christiansen
Choosing and Caring for a Shelter Dog: A Complete Guide to Help You Rescue and Rehome a Dog
Canine Learning Center, Publishing Division, 1996.

Liz Palika
Save That Dog!: Adopting a Purebred Rescue Dog
Hungry Minds, Incorporated, 1997.

Videos

Dog Lover's Guide to the Labrador Retriever
PetVisions Inc.
1010 Calle Negocio
San Clemente, CA 92673
(714) 498-7765

Periodicals

International Labrador Digest

Waterdog Publishing

Box 17158

Fayetteville, NC 28314

Fax (910) 487-9625.

Contact Lisa Tynan, *lisa4labs@aol.com*

$65 annual subscription domestic ($75 foreign),

6 issues per year.

International Labrador Newsletter

Contact Ken at *cranspire@compuserve.com*

or Penny Carpanini at *carpenny@atlas.co.uk*

Biannual, $10 per issue. Back issues available.

Mailing Lists

Labrador-L

Labrador-L is for people interested in Labrador Retrievers—1600 of them! To join, send email to *listserv@iupui.edu* and put subscribe LABRADOR-L your first name your last name in the body of the message. You will get an introductory Welcome file describing the general guidelines for the mailing list. The list is monitored but runs unmoderated.

Labrador-H

Hoflin Publications also runs Labrador-H, currently moderated by Jake Scott. This is a quieter list and also welcomes all those interested in Labradors. To join, send email to *requests@h19.hoflin.com* and put subscribe LABRADOR-H in the body of the message. Be sure to read Hoflin's agreement about ownership of posts to the list carefully!

LabsR4U

LabsR4U is a fully moderated list. To join, send email to *labsr4u-subscribe@egroups.com.* You will get an introductory Welcome file describing the general guidelines for the mailing list.

Websites

Labrador Retriever Homepage

www.k9web.com/breeds/l/labrador/

Working Retriever Central

www.working-retriever.com/

Ring of Labrador Retrievers

www.webring.org/cgi-bin/webring?ring=labs;list

Health Resources

Pet Emergency First Aid Videos

Apogee Videos has developed instructional videos on providing first aid to dogs and cats experiencing medical emergencies. More information about the videos and how to purchase them is available at *www.apogeevideo.com.*

Household Plant Reference from the ASPCA/APCC

67-page bound publication with sections on toxic, potentially toxic, and non-toxic plants. $15, including postage and handling. To obtain a copy please send your name and address along with a check for $15 to:

ASPCA Animal Poison Control Center
1717 South Philo Road
Suite #36
Urbana, IL 61802

Pet Loss Resources

Phone-in counseling is available through a number of veterinary colleges nationwide.

California

(530) 752-4200, or toll free (800) 565-1526—Staffed by University of California-Davis veterinary students; weekdays, 6:30-9:30 pm, Pacific Time (PT)

Florida

(352) 392-4700; then dial 1 and 4080—Staffed by University of Florida veterinary students; weekdays, 7:00-9:00 pm, Eastern Time (ET)

Illinois

(630) 603-3994—Staffed by Chicago VMA veterinarians and staffs. Leave voice-mail message; calls will be returned 7:00-9:00 pm, CT (Long-distance calls will be returned collect)

(217) 244-2273 or toll-free (877) 394-2273(CARE)—Staffed by University of Illinois veterinary students. Leave voicemail message; calls will be returned 7:00-9:00 pm (CT), Tuesdays, Thursdays, and Sundays.
net.cvm.uiuc.edu/CARE

Iowa

(888) ISU-PLSH—Pet Loss Support Hotline hosted by the Iowa State University College of Veterinary Medicine. Operational seven days a week, 6:00-9:00pm (CST) from Sept-April; Monday, Wednesday, Thursday from 6:00-9:00 pm (CST) from May-August.
www.vm.iastate.edu/support/

Maryland and Virginia

(540) 231-8038—Staffed by Virginia-Maryland Regional College of Veterinary Medicine; Tuesday, Thursday, 6:00-9:00 pm, (ET)

Massachusetts

(508) 839-7966—Staffed by Tufts University veterinary students; Tuesday, Thursday, 6:00-9:00 pm, (ET); voicemail messages will be returned daily, collect outside Massachusetts

Michigan

(517) 432-2696 Staffed by Michigan State University veterinary students; Tuesday to Thursday, 6:30-9:30 pm, (ET)

New York

(607) 253-3932—Cornell University Pet Loss Support Hotline staffed by Cornell University Veterinary Students Tuesday-Thursday 6:00-9:00 pm (ET), messages will be returned.

web.vet.cornell.edu/public/petloss/

Ohio

(614) 292-1823—Staffed by The Ohio State University veterinary students; Monday, Wednesday, Friday, 6:30-9:30 pm, (ET); voice-mail messages will be returned, collect, during operating hours

Washington

(509) 335-5704—Pet Loss Hotline, Washington State University, College of Veterinary Medicine.

www.vetmed.wsu.edu/plhl/index.htm

Index

G

H

I

O

P

Q

R

S

T

U

Photo Credits

Roger Boneham: p. 194

Sheila Boneham: p. 1; p. 11; p. 46; p. 86; p. 116

Booth Photography: p. 175

Keri Johnson: p. 199

Adrienne Rescinio: p. 83; p. 84; p. 85; p. 115

Tom Simms: p. 62

Karen Taylor: p. 61; p. 135; p. 200; p. 201

All other photos by Isabelle Francais

Cartoons by Michael Pifer